CLASS AND SOCIETY

STUDIES IN SOCIOLOGY

Consulting editor: Charles H. Page
University of
Massachusetts

CLASS and SOCIETY

Third Edition

Kurt B. Mayer
University of Bern, *Switzerland*
and
Walter Buckley
University of California, *Santa Barbara*

Random House NEW YORK

First Printing Third Edition

Library of Congress Catalog Card Number: 76–89481

Manufactured in the United States of America
by The Colonial Press Inc., Clinton, Massachusetts

Published, 1955
Third Edition, Revised and Reset, 1969

Design by Saul Schnurman

Preface to the Third Edition

Because of the very gratifying success this study has enjoyed since its first publication in 1955, the general approach and the order of presentation have been retained unchanged in this new, revised edition. At the same time, however, we have not only updated the empirical data but have also revised and considerably expanded the conceptual framework to take account of the many important contributions which have been added to the ever-expanding literature on social stratification during the last fifteen years.

Kurt B. Mayer
UNIVERSITY OF BERN,
SWITZERLAND

Walter Buckley
UNIVERSITY OF CALIFORNIA,
SANTA BARBARA

Contents

I Social Differentiation and Social Stratification 3

The Nature of Social Differentiation 3
Stratification as a Special Type of Social Differentiation 5
Stratification as a Pervasive Societal Phenomenon 9
Major Types of Stratification Systems in Complex Societies: Caste, Estate, Class 13

II Historical Development of Social Stratification 18

Stratification in Primitive Societies 18
Stratification in Ancient Societies 23

The Caste System of India 30
The Estate System of Medieval Europe 33

III Dimensions of Social Stratification in Modern Society 42

Class, Life Chances, and Class Consciousness 44
Status and Status Groups 46
Power 49
Social Mobility 50
A Model of the Perpetuation of Classes 51

IV Class in American Society: The Distribution of Life Chances 61

Differences in Income, Wealth, and Occupation 63
Class Differences in Life Expectancy, Health, and Mental Disorder 70
Class and Education 73
The Administration of Justice and Legal Protection 79
The Hierarchy of Classes 81

V Prestige, Style of Life, and Status Groups in American Society 86

Formal and Informal Associations and Participation 87
Value Orientations and Consumption Patterns 91

Family Patterns and Sexual Behavior 96
Racial, Ethnic, and Religious Distinctions and the Status System 102
Prestige and Stratification in the Local Community 107

VI The Structure of Power: Class, Formal Authority, and Informal Controls 109

Power and Control in American Communities 111
Is There a National Power Structure? 118

VII Class Awareness and Class Consciousness 125

Differences in Class Attitudes and Political Behavior 126
Class Identification and Class Consciousness 129
Status Awareness and Prestige Perspectives 132
Class Consciousness and the American Dream 134

VIII Social Mobility 137

Occupational Mobility 138
Status Mobility 143

The Encouragement and Restraint of Social Mobility 144
Social Mobility and Social Change: Stratification Trends in the United States 148

Notes 157

Selected Readings 173

Index 179

CLASS AND SOCIETY

I

Social Differentiation and Social Stratification

THE NATURE OF SOCIAL DIFFERENTIATION

Ever since men began to meditate and speculate about the nature of human society thousands of years ago, their attention has been drawn to the manifold differences that can readily be observed among human beings in every society. Some of these differences are biological variations, such as sex, age, size, mental capacity, and other traits inherent in the human organism. In addition to these inherited differences, the members of every society are further differentiated by many acquired social distinctions. Everywhere individuals differ from one another in occupation and possessions; in prestige and authority; in habits, interests, and cultural accomplishments; in tastes, attitudes, values, beliefs, and other acquired traits. All human societies take note of such individual differences. Some of these distinctions become the bases of different social positions and of different tasks in the organization of group activities and the patterns of daily living. This division of distinctive social roles and tasks, based upon both inherited and socially acquired individual differences, is called social *differentiation.*

Social differentiation is a universal characteristic of human societies. Early human societies survived and became dominant among animal species because of their superior social organization—that is, their more elaborate division of labor and consequent close coordination of activities. As individual animals, humans were not biologically superior; their strength and success lay in their superior intellect and language ability and the sociocultural organization that these made possible (and that in turn enhanced them). In the nonhuman world, on the other hand, differentiation is mainly determined by heredity: the division of labor is accomplished by physiological specialization of individual organisms that react in a relatively fixed, instinctive manner to stimuli provided by other organisms of the same species. Thus the whole intricate structure and detailed functional specialization of such insect societies as those of bees and ants are essentially a consequence of physiological differentiation. This does not hold true on the human level, however, where patterns of social behavior are shaped more specifically by culture than by the broader potentials provided by heredity. In human societies the coordination of individual efforts necessary for the preservation of the group is achieved through cultural specialization. The division of labor is accomplished by cultural means: individual members of society come, in one way or another, to fill the traditional positions and to acquire the different skills involved in the performance of the corresponding duties. Thus social differentiation is an integral aspect of human society. But as primitive societies gradually developed, there emerged out of the increasingly complex differentiation that particular kind of social organization that we refer to as *stratification.*

STRATIFICATION AS A SPECIAL TYPE OF SOCIAL DIFFERENTIATION

Individuals in the earliest primitive groups—where there was minimal division of labor—were socially distinguished largely on the basis of biological characteristics: sex, age, strength, and physical and psychological skills. Any invidious distinctions that were made tended to be in these terms. This meant that superior and inferior rankings of individuals could not be passed on by social inheritance but had to be acquired anew by each generation. Also, such groups, organized as they were almost entirely in terms of kinship relations, could not develop independent systems of social positions in which important invidious distinctions of rank could inhere. This is an important consideration, for—as we shall see—stratification emerges out of differentiation as distinctions of rank become attached to established social *positions,* rather than to individual, nontransferrable traits, and hence can be socially transmitted independently of innately endowed traits of inferiority or superiority.

This independence of innate "talents"—which are only potentials depending heavily on the social environment for their shaping and full realization—from recruitment of persons into social positions is shown clearly in the well-established fact that until very recent times such recruitment in all societies has taken place mainly on the basis of what sociologists have called ascription rather than achievement. That is, the positions individuals were to fill as adults were, within rather narrow limits, socially ascribed at birth and thus independent of any potential, or "innate," talents. This process apparently did not overly handicap most societies in their development since, as some anthropologists and sociologists have argued, most social positions in even the complex societies can quite adequately and

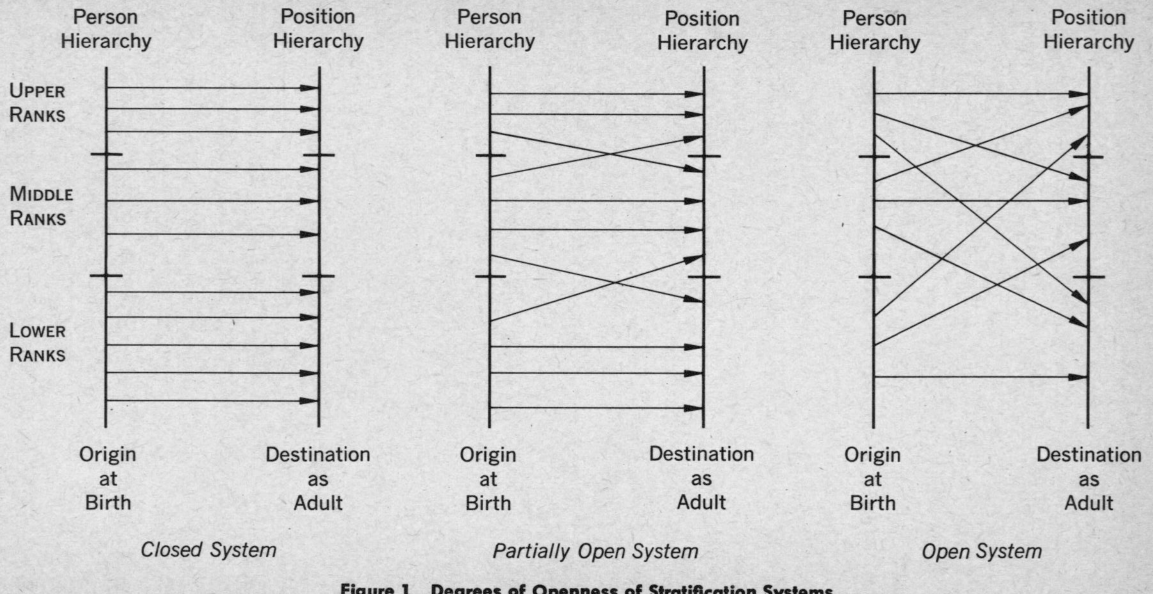

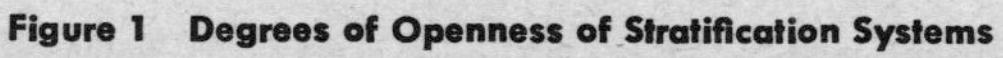

Figure 1 Degrees of Openness of Stratification Systems

conscientiously be filled by most individuals, given the training and social encouragement.[1] In contrast, some of the more recent societies are now characterized by an appreciable, though not predominant, degree of achievement of social positions. The concept of achievement implies, of course, adequate opportunities for the development of innate talents and a clear procedure for the testing and matching of such talents to the skill requirements of social positions. This poses the problem of "equality of opportunity" that has always been central to the study of social stratification.

Stratification, then, must be distinguished from the fact that individuals as well as social positions have always been differentiated to some degree in terms of invidious rankings. For social stratification refers to a particular relationship between individuals or subgroupings of a society and their recruitment into the particular hierarchy of social positions that have been conventionally established in that society. Thus the concept of stratification implies that there are two hierarchies that must be conceptually distinguished. First, when a society is stratified we find that individuals, families, and their subcultures may be arranged in a hierarchy on the basis of such criteria as wealth and income, prestige and styles of living, and power and authority. Second, we can distinguish a hierarchy of social, especially occupational, positions into which generations of individuals are recruited and from which they eventually retire. This hierarchy of positions is differentiated in terms of the resources—the material and psychological gratifications—and the power made available to those who hold them. The central focus of stratification study is the fact that, over a number of generations, those individuals who fill positions in any particular level of the positional hierarchy tend to be recruited from the corresponding level of the hierarchy of individuals and subgroups. That is, individuals tend to inherit the level of position they come to fill as adults through a complex of social, cultural, and psychological mechanisms and processes that we shall be discussing throughout the book (see Figure 1).

In sum, then, while all social differences may contain an invidious element and individual ranking is universal, most human societies beyond the earliest primitive groups have further elaborated the process of ranking (1) by arranging certain social positions in a graded hierarchy of socially superior and inferior ranks and (2) by arranging groupings of individuals and families into a related graded hierarchy such that these groupings tend to assume the same level of positions from generation to generation. Hence, whenever a society displays a graded series of ranked groupings of people more or less permanently matched over the generations to a graded hierarchy of social positions, we say that the society is stratified. Social stratification is thus a special type of social differentiation, signifying the existence of a more or less systematic hierarchy of social groupings matched in some degree to ranked social positions and thus treated as superior, equal, or inferior relative to one another in important social and material respects. Social *strata* are groupings of people who occupy positions of the same or similar rank. Such strata tend to pass on their ranks to their offspring through mechanisms of social inheritance.

The decline of such social inheritance in some societies during modern history suggests the theoretical possibility that future societies may retain a hierarchical ranking of positions differing to some degree in their command of wealth, status, and power, but may recruit persons into them in a way unaffected by any advantages of family position. Such a system is implied by the principle of equality of opportunity. However, sociological analysis indicates that this latter principle may be incompatible with the existing wide range of wealth, power, and status rankings of positions. It is important to consider whether a lower ceiling would have to be put on the wealth and power attached to social positions, and a much higher floor required. A basic question for research thus emerges: How wide may the range of differentials become without promoting significant advantages or disadvantages in the recruitment of new persons into social positions?

It is important to emphasize that stratification is primarily a *social* phenomenon, based on social and cultural *conventions* and the *authority* and *power* arrangements in the society. It cannot be adequately explained by innate biological or psychological characteristics of individuals and groups. The questions of whether stratification is inherent in the nature of society and whether it will be reduced to insignificance in the future will be discussed after we have examined the nature of stratification in greater detail.

It should also be clearly understood that not all social positions form part of a graded series of ranks. All Catholics do not form a social stratum, nor do all grandfathers, all Republicans, or all motorists, but we do consider aristocrats and manual laborers as forming social strata because these positions are part of a hierarchical gradation and command differentially graded resources and privileges.

STRATIFICATION AS A PERVASIVE SOCIETAL PHENOMENON

Hierarchical ranking into a number of strata, then, is but one way in which individuals may be socially differentiated; it did not mark the earliest societies and has developed in quite varying degrees in historical and recent societies. This poses two important questions: first, why do certain positions rather than others become stratified? and second, under what social conditions does social stratification arise? The answers to these questions are by no means entirely clear, but there seem to be several factors involved, all of which concern the relationship between social stratification and other elements of social organization.

Stratification is a pervasive societal phenomenon in that its historical development and its maintenance during any stable period involve some or all of the major institutional arrangements of society: family, political power organization, economics of production and distribution of wealth, distribution of knowledge and education, and so on. Thus it has been pointed out by several scholars[2] that one of the differences between stratified and unstratified positions hinges upon the role played by the family in the social ranking system. The family tends to be a well-integrated, intimate group. It not only procreates and rears children but also places them in the social order. At birth the child normally acquires the position of his family in the existing rank hierarchy. This placement function could not take place if the family did not form a unit with respect to the rank order, its members sharing the same rank and being treated as social equals. To be sure, sex, rank, and kinship differences within the family involve an invidious element—the head of the household has higher prestige than his dependents, and deference is due to elders on the part of children—but these invidious evaluations must not overly interfere with the proper functioning of the family unit. Therefore, those positions that are combined in the same family cannot, without strain, be made the basis of stratification; husbands and wives, parents and children, brothers and sisters, tend to belong to the same social stratum.

In the more complex and mobile societies, however, once the children of a household become adults and leave to take a job or start their own family, their status becomes more independent of that of their parents. Thus, in modern industrial societies of the East and West large numbers of persons have social positions and rank statuses quite different from those of their parents. Although there are a number of mechanisms tending to reduce the strains thus occurring, such as living in separate households often far apart, tensions often remain when social interaction occurs between, for example, lower-class parents and their more successful middle- or upper-class adult children and the latter's friends or associates. Such tensions reflect the degree to which class-based invidious distinctions have failed to decline with the increase of social mobility.

As we shall see in later sections, the family is also a central force underlying stratification because it is a primary socializing agent for most individuals. That is, it is a powerful force inculcating class-based attitudes, values, and social skills and determining the material and social resources available to individuals, all of which make for inequalities of opportunity and hence tend to underlie the perpetuation of social classes and the stratification system fostering them.

While age, sex, and kinship positions are nonstratified, those positions that give political authority or access to power over persons other than members of one's own family tend to become the main bases for stratification. By *power* we understand the ability to control the behavior of others. It is inherent in the nature of all organized human activity that some individuals are in a position to control in some degree the behavior of others. No human groups can function effectively unless some individuals perform the functions of coordinating and integrating the efforts of its members, thereby assuming the responsibilities of leadership, guidance, and control. The means by which guidance and control are exercised vary greatly, ranging from subtle influence and suggestion to the use of overt force and compulsion. But the exercise of power in whatever form usually commands prestige and reflects the existence of superiority-inferiority relationships.

The social positions that give access to power, however, can become bases of stratification only if power can be *institutionalized*. This is an important prerequisite. The possession of physical prowess, for example, or the wisdom of old age may entail power and command respect, but such powers and the resulting prestige are necessarily transitory and impermanent and cannot be converted into enduring rank. Permanence is an important characteristic of social stratification. Rank hierarchies, like everything human, are changeable, but they tend to be relatively stable and enduring. Only those positions, therefore, which permit the exercise of power based on durable criteria, such as the possession of valuable material goods or the control of nonmaterial values like magic formulas or religious symbols, can become the bases of persisting social strata.

In turn, the existence of social positions that permit the exercise of relatively permanent power and therefore the development of relatively stable rank hierarchies depends upon two factors: the numerical size of the group and the complexity of the group's economic organization. In very small primitive tribes that survive at a marginal level of subsistence the social organization often rests almost entirely on age, sex, and kinship divisions. Such tribes are so small numerically and their culture is so simple that no graded hierarchies of rank appear. There are differences in prestige and social influence, but these distinctions depend upon age, sex, and personal attributes, the exercise of power being casual in nature.[3]

The absence of social stratification among the smallest human societies has been admired by travelers who sometimes reported such cases to be a close approximation to a utopian state of perfect social equality. One must beware, however, of facile misinterpretations. The absence of social strata among the simplest tribes does not reflect the realization of any philosophical ideals of equality but simply the inability of any individual or group to convert personal prestige into relatively permanent social superiority. As L. T. Hobhouse put it long ago, "the savage enjoys freedom and equality, not because he has realized the value of these conceptions, but because neither he nor his fellow is strong enough to put himself above his neighbor." [4]

In addition to sheer size, the institutionalization of power and the establishment of permanent rank hierarchies depend upon the production of an economic surplus. Economic surplus refers to the production of goods in a quantity more than sufficient to assure the continuous physical existence of all members of the group. So long as a society remains close to the bare level of subsistence, no individual can control much more than an equal share of its material wealth. The productive resources are the property of all members of the group. But as technological skills become sufficiently advanced to produce more than a subsistence minimum, the economic surplus tends to be allocated unequally: it is claimed by individuals of outstanding abilities in hunting, fishing, or warfare, as well as by those who perform special services with respect to the supernatural. The respect and prestige that special abilities and unusual exploits command among humans provide the necessary social recognition of the claims advanced by specific individuals and groups to a larger share of the economic surplus. This condition permits the accumulation of individual fortunes and results in the unequal distribution of wealth.

Since wealth is durable and property transmissible, they provide a convenient basis for the institutionalization of personal prestige. The control of wealth makes it possible to perpetuate power and to transform individual differences in prestige and influence into hereditary hierarchies of rank. Consequently, as substantial numerical size and an economic surplus are attained, rudimentary equality tends to give way to unmistakable social stratification.[5]

MAJOR TYPES OF STRATIFICATION SYSTEMS IN COMPLEX SOCIETIES: CASTE, ESTATE, CLASS

Although most societies that have progressed beyond the hunting and gathering level of subsistence are stratified, concrete forms of rank hierarchy vary greatly from society to society. Cultural variations stimulate different forms of stratification so that ranking systems differ markedly from time to time and from one society to another. In concrete fact, then, there are as many different forms of stratification as there are human societies.

Despite the manifold variations, we may distinguish three general types of stratification: systems of *caste, estate,* and *class.* Before depicting each of these types, it should be stressed that they are "pure"—that is, abstract—types. Concrete systems of stratification never occur in pure form, but merely approximate a given type. Moreover, most systems represent a mixture of types.

In a pure *caste* system the social strata consist of closed social groups, arranged in a fixed order of superiority and inferiority. An individual is born into a particular caste and must stay there for the rest of his life. He acquires his social position with its accompanying rights and obligations from his parents and cannot change his rank through personal qualities or achievements. There being no provision for individual social mobility, the individual cannot rise or fall in the caste system, not even through intermarriage, for the castes are endogamous. A caste system represents the most rigid type of social stratification. In its fully developed form it has been approximated only in India (see Chapter II), but castelike or quasi-caste systems have occurred in various societies whenever social strata have tended to evolve into closed, endogamous groups.

The second type of stratification system, that of *estates,* typically occurs in feudal societies where social organization revolves around a specific form of land tenure—that is, where land is held on condition of military service and a man's social position depends on his relationship to the land. An estate system consists of a hierarchy of several social strata, which are clearly distinguished and rigidly set off from one another by law and custom. Characteristically, estate systems manifest general hierarchical arrangements: At the top stands a royal family and a landholding, hereditary military aristocracy, closely followed by an allied priesthood, ranking on a par with the secular nobility. Below them are merchants and craftsmen, while free peasants and unfree serfs form the broad bottom strata. Each estate has clearly defined rights and duties, and social position is usually inherited. Individuals may legally change their estates, however, under certain circumstances. Thus the king may confer a title of nobility on a commoner, or the daughter of a wealthy merchant may marry into the aristocracy. To be sure, marriages between persons of different estate are rare, but they are not absolutely prohibited as in a caste system. Then too, a serf may be freed by his master or an exceptionally bright peasant lad may advance his rank by entering the priesthood or the military service, both of which function as channels of upward mobility. Estates, then, are less rigid than castes, but since this form of stratification usually is based upon a stable agricultural economy, estate systems tend to be static and fixed. Hereditary transmission of social position is the general rule and social mobility, though possible within the legal definitions of the systems, is difficult and limited. A more detailed discussion of estates will be found in Chapter II, where the historical development of this system in medieval Europe is outlined.

Finally, in a *class* system, the social hierarchy is based primarily upon differences in monetary wealth and income. Social classes are not sharply marked off from each other, nor are they demarcated by tangible boundaries. Unlike estates, they have no legal standing, individuals of all classes being in principle equal before the law. Consequently there are no legal restraints on the movement of individuals and families from one class to another. The same is true of intermarriage which, while it may be frowned upon and informally discouraged, is not usually prevented by law or insuperable social pressures. Unlike castes, social classes are not necessarily organized, closed social groups. Rather they are aggregates of persons with similar amounts of wealth and property and similar sources of income. Nevertheless, they may be analytically separated into statistically significant subgroups or subcultures in terms of such criteria as interaction patterns, political attitudes, and life styles.

In societies marked by a class system the differences in wealth and income are expressed in different ways of life: patterns of consumption, types of education, speech, manners, dress, tastes, and other cultural attributes. In turn, these differences give rise to the formation of *status groups*. These are informal social groups whose members view each other as equals because they share common understandings—as expressed in similar attitudes and similar modes of behavior—and who treat or regard outsiders as social superiors or inferiors. Thus in a class society there develops a hierarchy of status groups that is interrelated but not identical with the hierarchy of economic classes. The reciprocal and changing relationships between classes and status groups result in a highly complex stratification structure. This complexity poses difficult conceptual problems in the analysis of class systems, which will be treated in some detail in Chapter III. Moreover, a large part of this study is devoted to the description and analysis of a major concrete case, the contemporary American class structure.

Here it is sufficient to state in summary fashion that as a general type class systems are less rigid than caste or estate systems. The different classes, and to a lesser degree the status groups, are relatively permeable. There is a considerable amount of movement up and down the class and status hierarchies. Although the individual acquires his initial position at birth, ascription does not necessarily determine his later social rank, which can be changed through the acquisition or loss of wealth and other attainments. As a result, class societies are apt to be highly competitive and fluid, since individuals and families may compete for wealth and social position on the basis of personal qualities and achievements.

In tracing the development of stratification from its emergence out of the earliest settled agricultural societies to its present condition in the most complex industrial societies, a very general pattern may be discerned. As earlier small-scale societies gave rise to the larger complex ancient civilizations, the degree and rigidity of stratification increased at a rapid pace. With the beginnings of the modern world in the West this pace leveled off, and then began a decline that picked up rapid momentum as the West, and somewhat later the East, entered the contemporary era of large-scale industrialism. Measured in almost any terms, such societies have shown a significant decrease in the scale and rigidity of the stratification system—a decline that must seem of enormous proportions when compared against the ancient civilizations, such as those of Egypt, India, Greece, China, and Rome, with their huge majorities of submerged or culturally marginal members.

Considerations of this broad trend inevitably lead to the question of how far and how fast societies can continue to go toward a fully unstratified condition. Such a question is not only of practical concern, since many societies are now grappling seriously with it; but it is also an important problem for the purely sociological imagination, since it demands answers to the theoretical questions of what such a society would look like and whether the latter is indeed possible (or even, as a few would have it, has not already been attained).

The conceptualization of stratification that we have presented above suggests some broad outlines: An unstratified society, while being marked by some rank differences of social positions and of individuals and subgroupings, would show no significant correlation between social positions of individuals at birth and their adult positions in the formal and informal organizations of society. This situation implies rather full equality of opportunity, in terms of psychological and social as well as material advantages. But full equality in turn implies a somewhat restricted range of differentials in the rankings of persons and of social—especially occupational—positions, particularly with respect to amounts and types of transferrable wealth and power associated with these ranks. That is, as we suggested above, lack of stratification implies a fairly high floor on the share of resources available to all persons, and perhaps a more modest ceiling as well—at least compared to what is now possible for a few. But what would a restricted range of this kind imply for the motives of individuals, the values of groups, and the institutional arrangement of society?

These are intriguing sociological questions. We raise them at the outset because, implicitly at least, they will face us all along. But at the end of the book we shall have only begun to appreciate their intricacies. For the study of social stratification leads to the analysis of the whole of society as a complex, ever-changing system of intricately interrelated parts.

II

Historical Development of Social Stratification

A brief account of the development of social stratification in primitive and earlier historical times will serve to make the abstract analysis of the preceding chapter more concrete.

STRATIFICATION IN PRIMITIVE SOCIETIES

Recent work of a number of anthropologists has led to a view of primitive societies as analyzable into at least three levels on a scale of degrees of stratification: traditional or equalitarian society, open or rank society, and stratified society.[1]

Societies of the *traditional* or *equalitarian* type consisted of small bands of wandering hunters and gatherers varying in size from about thirty to something over one hundred. The level of technology was low, permitting no significant economic surplus of goods. Social organization consisted primarily of a close web of kinship, and social differentiation or division of labor was slight and based on biological characteristics such as age, sex, or special personal attributes. Graded hereditary ranks were ascribed to individuals on the basis of kinship and biological or personal traits, but these were noncompetitive and could not result in the division of the society into class subgroupings. There were as many positions of rank as there were persons to fill them, so that all had some rank and no invidious subgroup distinctions could arise and be perpetuated. There was no significant economic inequality and no regular surplus to compete for or fight over. The demands for survival put a premium on close cooperation and mutual support, and the "seamless web of kinship" was well adapted to these requirements.

As societies increased their technology or for other reasons were able to exploit their environment more successfully and produce some surplus of goods, population tended to increase and social organization to become more complex. Under such conditions the *open* or *rank* society was apt to develop, in which status rivalry and competition or conflict over the distribution of surplus goods intensified to a point where leadership came to depend more on political prowess and force than on traditional hereditary seniority. Traditional rank continued to exist, but it no longer assured actual leadership in group activities and decision-making. In the typical case, warriors have assumed so much power that status lineages have regrouped around them or around competing political leaders and the traditional order of seniority has been at least partially broken. Such power groups are held together more by material considerations of self-advancement and safety than by claims of kinship.

The open society tends to be a transitional type of society characterized by a fluid situation of shifting subgroup allegiances and claims, as competing or conflicting subgroups vie for support and power. Though there is no economic stratification into clear-cut subgroupings based on material inequalities, there is a social or prestige system of stratification dividing the population into, for example, a servant class, "low people," "honorable commoners," "lesser nobility," and the like.

Stratified society tended to develop out of the transitional open society as rivalries and conflicts gave way to the dominance of one or more groups over others and rank differences of such subgroups became institutionalized. Dominant political and economic groupings, bolstered by control of much of the institutional apparatus of the society and by the support of religious and other cultural legitimizing groupings, have replaced the earlier traditional web of kinship. Social cleavage of the society into recognizable economic and prestige-ranked groupings is now regarded by members as unbridgeable. Sometimes the very subsistence of certain groups becomes an issue in political conflict. All material and cultural resources may be put to use in greater struggles.

A key change in institutional arrangements revolved around land tenure: a clear distinction tended to develop between the landed and the landless, a situation usually resulting from political expropriation of commoners' land previously held by traditional hereditary right. In more advanced cases, such as Tahiti and Hawaii (in their aboriginal developed state), administrative divisions replaced the older and traditional organization of lineage and tribe. Primitive stratified society was appreciably larger in population and territory and more sophisticated in material and administrative technology than the traditional equalitarian society.

There are socially and sociologically strategic differences between traditional and stratified primitive societies. In the traditional case, there are enough ranks to go around and no individuals or subgroups are second-class members. Rank differences, furthermore, do not lead to significant economic distinctions in the distribution of goods. And, most important, the fact that ranks are based on hereditary kin relations, plus the extensive web of kinship ties, means that ranks are distributed in a diffuse way throughout the society such that no one or two subgroupings monopolize them. Hence there is no development of subgroups (for example, classes or castes) based on invidious rank distinctions.

In the stratified primitive society, on the other hand, many or most of the members have no significant rank. In addition, rank distinctions go hand in hand with economic distinctions, especially between the landed and the landless, with the material existence of lower groups sometimes subject to the arbitrary decisions of the upper. Distinctive subgroups (class or caste) develop, based on economic, political, and prestige differences that override the integrating web of kinship. That is, unbridgeable cleavages develop around *institutionalized* inequalities such that class subgroups which have unequal access to advantaged positions are perpetuated over the generations by various social, psychological, and cultural mechanisms.

These institutional mechanisms and their functions are clearly shown by the anthropologist Marshall Sahlins in his study of stratification in fourteen independent island societies of Polynesia. These societies all derived in early primitive times from a common culture base on one of the islands, but later, groups split off from the original culture and migrated to the various islands to develop their societies independently. Over a number of generations the separate societies evolved in different ways, and one important variable that emerged was the degree to which they became stratified. It was found that generally, as productivity increased and a surplus of goods became possible, a wider and wider social distinction developed between those persons who produced goods and those who controlled their distribution. This distinction came to correspond to the social difference between chief and nonchief, which in turn ramified into other aspects of culture.

The societies of the Polynesian islands were divided into three main groups according to their degree of stratification. The group containing the most highly stratified societies included Hawaii, Tonga, Samoa, and Tahiti. The least stratified group included Pukapuka, Ontang Java, and Takelau. Let us look at these two extreme groups, labeled I and III by Sahlins, in terms of some of the key structures or social mechanisms underlying the institutionalization of a stratified system. In Group I (the highly stratified group) Sahlins found a structurally complex ranking system, with usually three status levels; whereas in Group III there were at best two status levels, with very few members in the upper. Group I chiefs enjoyed a preeminent stewardship, with control of communal production and redistribution of goods and with authority to inflict severe punishments for violation of resource rights and ability to confiscate goods of others by force in some cases. In Group III, on the other hand, resources were vested mainly in kin-group heads and most distribution was by reciprocal exchange between kin groups. Violations of resource rights were usually supernaturally punished.

A large range of clothes, ornaments, and the like served as insignia of rank within Group I societies, and chiefs did not engage in their own subsistence activities. In Group III societies there were almost no insignia of rank and in only one case did the chief not produce his own subsistence. High chiefs in Group I enjoyed an arbitrary despotism, with control over the social regulatory processes; there were also clear differences by status in the ability to inflict secular punishment on wrongdoers, including the ability to kill or banish. Such arbitrary powers by chiefs were lacking in Group III societies, where elders and kin heads controlled the socioregulatory processes. Status differences did not relate to the punishment of wrongdoers, and there was strong dependence on supernatural rather than secular sanctions.

Group I societies maintained very complex tabu systems concerning the upper-status level: endogamous marriages among chiefly families were strictly enforced; elaborate postures of obeisance and respect were insisted upon; and spectacular rites for all life crises of high chiefs were held. For Group III societies there were fewer respect forms and tabus concerning chiefs and only a slight elaboration of chiefly life-crisis rites.

Only a vague tendency toward marriage between persons with prestige was found.

These contrasts show how a stratified social system, once established, tends to elaborate and maintain itself as a self-perpetuating system. And to reemphasize the definition of stratification presented in Chapter I, we see that stratification implies not simply the differentiation of persons and groups in terms of varying ranks and social positions, but the creation of relatively distinct subcultures with arbitrarily—that is, institutionally—defined differential access to goods and social positions, which are thus perpetuated over the generations.

STRATIFICATION IN ANCIENT SOCIETIES

In all likelihood social stratification did not appear among prehistoric societies until the great innovations of farming and stock-raising occurred in the Neolithic period, just prior to the dawn of recorded history. The domestication and breeding of animals and the raising of crops represented a revolutionary advance in man's struggle for survival, making possible permanent village settlements and some assurance of subsistence, as well as a chance of economic surplus. The sedentary life and the economic increment enabled those who served in the capacity of priests and soothsayers to free themselves from the necessity of raising their own food. Thus spiritual leaders gradually gained control over the economic surplus and consolidated their prestige and power, setting themselves apart from the rest of the village population.

This incipient social stratification was greatly furthered by the development of town life, which began in the late Neolithic period some seven or eight thousand years ago. The most spectacular features of prehistoric towns and of the cities of the earliest historical era were the temple structures that dominated the local communities. These temples were houses for gods, of course, but they were also the abodes of the divine servants, the priests. Only a good-sized population could supply the materials and labor necessary for their construction, and the work had to be well coordinated and carefully planned. Clearly there were those who gave orders and those who obeyed: the earliest historical records give evidence of the existence of well-organized priesthoods more than five thousand years ago. The priests claimed the economic surplus in the name of their gods, directing the temple building and other public works on which the surplus wealth was expended.[2] They exercised both religious and secular powers, forming a ruling class of priest-chiefs that stood at the apex of society in early Mesopotamia, Egypt, and other ancient civilizations. Their power rested on the firm belief of the entire population that supernatural assistance was necessary in the difficult struggle against the adversities and misfortunes of human life and on the corollary conviction that the mediation of the priests was required to obtain this superhuman assistance.

However, another class soon arose, which was able to claim a substantial share of the surplus and establish itself alongside the priests. As the wealth of the towns and the surrounding countryside increased, it had to be protected from raids of marauding nomads and envious neighbors. In time this essential function came to be performed by a class of professional warriors who, like the priests, were supported by the underlying population. The military class eventually developed into an aristocracy of warrior-nobles and court officials who assumed the secular functions of government and who were headed by a king or "king of kings." The rise of the military aristocracy sometimes resulted in clashes with the priestly class, but usually the two groups formed an alliance of common rule.

At the base of the social hierarchy of early civilizations was the large mass of peasants, the tillers of the soil, who created and replenished the surplus that went into the hands of the priestly and military rulers. The status of the peasants varied from age to age and in different lands. Some were free peasants, paying taxes; others were landless agricultural laborers. Many were serfs, bound to the land which they could not leave and were obligated to work. Serfs were also subject to enforced labor on roads, canals, and other public works. Still others were slaves who could be bought, sold, loaned, and pledged (although, like all established groups, they possessed *some* rights, at least in principle).

Although some form of serfdom seems to have been imposed upon most, if not all, tillers of the soil in very early times both in Mesopotamia and in Egypt, their social status probably deteriorated as civilization advanced. As the techniques of cultivation improved and economic surplus grew larger, ruling classes became more powerful and ambitious and tightened their control of the peasantry, draining away from them everything above the barest minimum necessary for subsistence. By imperceptible degrees the dependence and subordination of the peasants increased. The growth of cities and the development of empires provided larger markets, making agricultural production more profitable. Not only the crown and the temples, but private landlords also acquired large landed estates, which were farmed for profit, managed by overseers, and worked by serfs or slaves. Some free peasants acquired sufficient land to rise to the ranks of the landed aristocracy but many others became landless agricultural laborers, and serfs and slaves increased in number.

Whatever their specific legal status, the living conditions of the tillers of the soil were very similar everywhere in antiquity: their techniques of cultivation were crude, their productivity was low, and their daily round of activities differed little from that of their Neolithic ancestors. The only major change was that an ever-larger portion of their product was used to maintain the growing urban and economically dependent elements of the population.[3]

This urban population soon became further subdivided into several social strata as an increasing number of persons were withdrawn from direct food production to the performance of more specialized tasks. Growing economic specialization and the development of industrial technology created three distinct new urban classes: a small middle class of professional merchants and traders, an urban working class of craftsmen and artisans, and a large class of slaves.

The middle class of merchants, traders, and business enterprisers grew slowly, becoming an important stratum comparatively late in the development of civilization. Although the archeological record gives evidence of the early existence of traders, they did not figure very largely in the earliest periods of urban life, mainly because the function of economic enterprising was originally the monopoly of the temple priesthoods. But with the emergence of the military class, industry and trade became a function of the secular government. The chief entrepreneur was the king, especially in ancient Egypt, where economic enterprises were traditionally controlled by the ruling dynasties and independent merchants had relatively little scope. In Mesopotamia merchants appeared at first under royal patronage but later acquired independence and began to play an important role. For example, in Babylon wealthy merchants possessed great establishments with numerous employees of all sorts; Babylonian businessmen eventually became a major factor in the community, rivaling the power of the priestly and the military classes. With the rise of a money economy late in the imperial age, shipowners, merchants, and bankers played prominent roles in the commercial cities, and in Phoenician society the businessmen constituted the political ruling class.

Specialized craftsmen and industrial workers appear first on the historical scene in the temple household establishments where they worked under the supervision of the priests, upon whom they depended for food and shelter. In early Egypt they were attached to the great royal household, deriving sustenance from the royal granaries and being supplied with tools and raw materials from the king's stocks. Other artisans were permanently attached to temples and to the landed estates of the nobility. Artisans seem to have had little personal freedom, probably changing hands with the estates on which they worked, much like the peasant serfs. However, since each craft developed techniques that required learning before they could be practiced, the artisans were able to organize in guilds under their own leaders for the protection of their common interests. Nevertheless, production was carried on for the household use of the landed estates and not for the market, and thus Egyptian craftsmen could not achieve an independent position in society.[4]

In contrast, production for the market in Mesopotamia seems to have begun early, giving rise to an urban class of artisans. In Babylon urban craftsmen were no longer attached to great households but subsisted independently. As cities grew and civilization expanded in the later imperial age, craft products and manufactures were in great demand for export purposes as well as for local consumption. Besides the highly skilled craftsmen there also developed in the Babylonian and Phoenician cities considerable bodies of less-specialized workingmen, probably creating for the first time in history an urban working class divorced from the land.[5] The legal status of artisans and other urban workingmen differed, many being legally free citizens while others were slaves and formed a part of the numerically large class of town slaves.

The origins of slavery are not clear, but its commonest source undoubtedly lay in the enslavement of prisoners of war. In prehistoric societies war captives were usually put to death because nomadic hunting tribes, who lived from hand to mouth, had little use for the services of slaves. But in technologically more advanced, sedentary societies it was clearly advantageous to spare some or all of the captives since their labor could be put to productive use. Alien slaves could be ordered to do all sorts of things that native men and women would not do so willingly. Moreover, slavery was an effective form of exploitation, since the entire product of slave labor, above the barest minimum necessary for survival, could be appropriated by the master. Thus, as civilization became more complex and the demand for labor power rose, slavery grew rapidly. Slaves were set to work on farms and public works, in households, mines, and workshops, and slavery became a major social institution in all ancient urban cultures. The ranks of the slaves were swelled not only by war and conquest but by heredity, debt, and crime. Children of slaves became slaves by birth, and debtors who could not discharge their debts either fell into slavery themselves or sold their wives and children. In some cases slavery was the prescribed penalty for crime.

The treatment and the social status of slaves varied widely, depending largely upon their skill and occupation. Those who were craftsmen and possessed skills in some trade were relatively well treated. The condition of the town slaves was not abject. In later Babylon, for example, their social position was carefully defined and their lives were legally protected under the code of Hammurabi. They had the right to acquire and own property and could buy their freedom, as many of them did, thereby becoming freemen who worked for wages. On the other hand, slaves who tended fields, orchards, and flocks were simple laborers, receiving little food and even less clothing. The hardest lot of all, however, was that of "gang slaves" who pulled the oars of galleys, worked in mines, dug canals, and erected temples, walls, and embankments. Their treatment was extremely harsh, they were sometimes literally worked to death, and at best their working conditions, in modern terms, were inhuman. Their labor furnished the motive power of a civilization without mechanical energy.

In time slaves came to form a large proportion of the population in all ancient lands, slave labor furnishing the chief basis of support for the complex societies of Babylonia, Egypt, Assyria, Greece, and Rome.

The pattern of social stratification, which grew up gradually in the course of five or six thousand years in the great river valleys of the Near East, has been sketched in very broad outline. Specific features of the stratification system varied in detail from one society to another and from time to time. But the basic patterns of the social structure remained essentially the same throughout antiquity. The social hierarchy was everywhere dominated by the priest class and the military aristocracy; only late in the imperial age were these two strata joined and rivaled in some places by a powerful class of businessmen who founded a merchant aristocracy. Although numerically small, the ruling classes possessed the means of military power, wealth, and intellectual leadership, which they used for the accumulation and concentration of an ever-larger economic surplus that was expended almost entirely on the satisfaction of their own wants and for the perpetuation of their own prestige and power. The millions of peasants, urban workers, serfs, and slaves had little or no share in the wealth that they produced; their energy was used to create a highly developed material civilization, from which they derived small benefit.

One of the most significant consequences of the exclusion of the working classes from the refinements of civilization was the intellectual dualism that accompanied the invention of writing. Writing was first developed by the priests as a means of keeping accounts of temple revenues and of recording economic rights and obligations. Like most of the features of urban civilization, writing had its origin in the new circumstances created by the formation of the economic surplus, serving the ruling and possessing classes as a convenient instrument to entrench their property rights and to perpetuate their power. Peasants and artisans, on the other hand, had little or no chance to learn the new art of writing, which was cumbersome and complicated and required specialized training and formal education. Literacy was thus confined to those who did not engage in manual labor. The small minority who knew writing developed in time an intellectual tradition of learning and formal erudition that differed fundamentally from the intellectual life of the illiterate masses, whose beliefs and social attitudes remained "primitive" in orientation and content.

This intellectual dualism greatly intensified the gulf dividing the social classes of ancient society. As time went on, the economic, social, and cultural cleavage between ruling classes, urban workers, and rural masses tended to harden. Each of these classes developed its own way of life and reared its children in its own fashion. The separation of classes became clear, distinct, and continuous. The ruling classes recognized no kinship with the masses from whom they set themselves off sharply, refusing intermarriage. The artisans, in turn, developed guild organizations within which both the practice of their craft and the marriage of their members were concentrated. At various periods, for example during the Egyptian Middle Kingdom, social classes tended to become closed orders, taking on the character of hereditary estates.[6]

But the tendencies toward closure and exclusiveness never developed fully for any considerable length of time; mobility of individuals from one class to another and intermarriage were never completely barred. Thus individuals of different class origins were permitted to acquire a knowledge of writing in the schools conducted by the temples, and in later Egypt boys seem to have had some choice between formal schooling, agricultural work, and apprenticeship to a craft.[7] Moreover, the class hierarchy itself was frequently disturbed by historical developments and major cultural innovations, illustrated by the new methods of producing wealth and of exercising military power which repeatedly altered the relative positions of social classes. Conquests, wars, and invasions often changed the composition of the ruling classes, as invaders tended to replace native rulers. In addition, the introduction of bronze and iron seems to have weakened the priestly classes everywhere and strengthened the military aristocracies, while the mastery of writing greatly helped the merchant classes to emerge as an important social element.[8] We may conclude, then, that although class divisions were sharp and pronounced in antiquity the early systems of social stratification never developed the fixity and rigidity that characterized the caste system that arose in India.

THE CASTE SYSTEM OF INDIA

The origins of the Indian caste system are not at all clear, but many competent scholars hold that it resulted from the penetration of the Indian subcontinent by Indo-European tribes who called themselves Aryans. Invading India from the northwest in a number of tribal waves, the Aryans met and conquered native Dravidian tribes, darker in complexion and possessing a different culture, with whom they subsequently intermixed. From the process of conquest, intermixture, and settlement (which is unrecorded by history), the Aryan priests, or Brahmans, in time emerged as the dominant social element. In the pursuit of their own interests, the Brahmans appear to have gradually transformed the formerly simple tribal social structure into the rigid and complex system of social stratification which has existed in India for thousands of years and which has come down into modern times almost intact.

The first literary records of the caste system are to be found in the *Vedas,* a collection of hymns that were probably composed about the middle of the second millennium B.C. Constituting the fundamental holy books of Hinduism, they describe the divine creation of a hierarchy of four principal castes (the Hindu word is *varna*). At the top stood the *Brahmans,* who were the priests and teachers of the sacred lore. It was their duty to uphold the social order under divine guidance. The *Kshatryias,* or warriors who formed the military aristocracy, included princely rulers whose function was the protection of social order and the sacred lore. Like the Brahmans, they had the right to wear the sacred thread, the symbol of spiritual rebirth and ritual purity. The *Vaisyas,* the third large caste, were peasants, craftsmen, and merchants who were also ritually pure and shared the right to wear the sacred thread. The *Sudras,* who performed manual labor and menial services of all sorts, constituted the lowest caste; their duty was to serve the three higher castes peaceably. The Sudras were not considered ceremonially pure and were not permitted to wear the symbolic sacred thread. Outside and below the castes were all the tribes not included in the Hindu spiritual community—the outcastes.

It should be realized that this ancient fourfold classification is neither a scientific description nor a historical account of the caste system, but rather represents a picture of Indian society as seen from the point of view of the Brahmans. It is a mythological rationalization developed by the dominant priests which has served to keep the other castes in their assigned places.

The Hindu social system probably never consisted of only four castes. At any rate, these traditional divisions have long since been complicated and overlaid by innumerable subdivisions into a multitude of several thousand different castes which mark the social structure of contemporary India.

These numerous castes, in principle and largely in practice, are mutually exclusive social groups. Membership in the caste being hereditary and fixed for life, there is almost no social mobility except through transmigration of souls. Members may neither eat nor intermarry with persons of a lower caste. The castes are kept strictly isolated from each other by a web of customs and ceremonials that govern the minutiae of everyday life, holding the members of each caste to one definite way of living and to one group of associates. In the past each caste was also united by a hereditary occupation and had a well-organized governing body, which enforced caste regulations and maintained strict discipline. Caste has been the Alpha and Omega of Hindu life, the greatest sin being to "lose caste." A person who does so by violating the caste regulations is ostracized and may become an outcaste.

The customary way of life determines the social prestige of a caste and its position in the caste hierarchy. Each caste has its particular rank in the social order, which it strives to maintain or improve. Its position in the rank hierarchy is defined by the expressed or assumed opinions and attitudes of the Brahmans, who rank at the top and set the standards of respectability. Other castes are graded downward according to their social distance from the Brahmans. The caste system as a whole thus represents a successful imposition, largely by means of religious rituals, of the overlordship of the Brahmans on all other social classes. It is essentially a religious order hinging upon the indispensability of the services of a hereditary, exclusive priesthood. Economically, the system involves the exploitation of a large number of depressed or "unclean" and "untouchable" castes who form a submerged fifth of the total population, living in abject poverty. Although its precise form has changed from time to time, the caste system has endured for over three thousand years. It is the most thoroughgoing attempt known to human history to establish a stable social structure based entirely on inherited social distinctions.

There is unmistakable evidence, however, that under the impact of industrialization, urbanization, and Westernization, the caste system is beginning to crumble. Developed in a slowly changing, agricultural village society, the caste system is ill-adapted to the rapidly changing conditions of modern urban-industrial life. In today's factories and schools and on modern transportation systems members of various castes are inevitably forced to come into close physical contact. As a result, many of the religious prohibitions against such intermingling are now breaking down. Moreover, this trend is hastened by the declared policy of the present Indian government, which endeavors to abolish and outlaw all economic and educational discrimination practiced against "untouchables" and to foster a greater degree of equality of opportunity for all Indians, regardless of caste. However, the government is not trying to abolish the caste system as such, and many of its restrictions persist. Thus the prohibition against intercaste marriage, a vital part of the whole system, is still seldom violated, even in the cities. Therefore it would be premature to expect the total disappearance of the caste system in the near future, in spite of the considerable modifications now taking place.

THE ESTATE SYSTEM OF MEDIEVAL EUROPE

The extreme rigidity of the Indian caste system was never fully equaled in the Western world. But the disintegration of urban civilization which accompanied and followed the decline of the Roman Empire did give rise to fundamental changes in the pattern of social stratification that had arisen with and been anchored in the urban cultures of antiquity. The dissolution of the Roman state and the breakup of the economic system of the ancient world which followed the Germanic invasions of the West and the rise of Islam brought about an interruption of commerce and transportation, resulting in the disappearance of the merchants and the decline of towns and cities. By the end of the eighth century of the Christian Era Western Europe had returned to an almost purely agricultural economy.[9]

These economic and political changes were accompanied by a transformation of the social structure. As the urban way of life decayed and finally disappeared it was replaced by a new rural social order that was based mainly on the possession of land. Land became almost the sole source of subsistence for all segments of the population: everyone, from king to humblest peasant, lived directly or indirectly off the land, whether he personally cultivated the soil or confined himself to collecting and consuming its products.[10] In this rural society prestige and power depended essentially on the individual's hereditary relationship to the land. Those who possessed land were free and powerful, while others were dependent both economically and politically.

In the feudal regime which emerged from the Carolingian empire and spread over most of Europe after the ninth century, a small minority of lay and ecclesiastical proprietors controlled great landed estates that were cultivated by large numbers of tenants, most of whom were serfs or quasi-serfs. The feudal social hierarchy recognized a fundamental division of society into three well-defined strata: nobility, clergy, and peasantry. Each of these divisions constituted a definite segment of society, an *estate,* which was separated from the other strata by custom and social attitudes and by formally defined legal rights and duties that were both expressed in theory and upheld in practice. (The conception of estates did not really arise in medieval Europe until late in the thirteenth century, but the conditions on which the concept was based had been developing for hundreds of years.) Social and legal distinctions between the three estates were clear-cut. The nobility was a military aristocracy charged with the defense of the country and the exercise of judicial power. The clergy, an ecclesiastical and intellectual elite, not only ministered to the spiritual needs of the population but, as the only literate stratum in the early medieval period, also performed important administrative functions. The peasantry's principal social obligation was to labor for the support of the nobility and the clergy, who dominated the feudal hierarchy. During the earlier part of the Middle Ages, these two groups enjoyed a virtual monopoly of wealth, social prestige, and political power.

Originally the nobility was set off from the other strata of medieval society not by legal barriers but by its landed wealth, its military profession, and a distinctive style of life, which disdained direct manual labor. Gradually, however, and largely due to the pressure exercised by a newly rising group of rich town merchants who invested their profits in landed estates, the military aristocracy attempted to transform itself into a legally closed estate.[11] After the twelfth century, entrance into the nobility could be obtained only through heredity or royal grace; henceforth the king alone could elevate a person of non-noble birth to the closed ranks of the nobility. During the height of the Middle Ages kings made but sparing use of this power, though in later centuries patents of nobility were granted with increasing frequency to those who could afford to pay a substantial monetary consideration for the privilege.

Despite these tendencies toward closure, however, the feudal nobility was not a socially homogeneous estate. On the contrary, in every country definite gradations of rank existed within the aristocracy, distinguished by a series of characteristic titles. A noble's status derived largely from the size of his landed estates and the number of dependents and retainers whose services he could command. Ordinarily the feudal noble was a vassal, holding his land as a grant, or fief, from the king or from another noble on condition of military service and various other obligations. The relationship between lord and vassal was originally personal and contractual, providing for the vassal's performance of specified duties in return for protection and livelihood. The latter usually took the form of a land grant, but by the ninth or tenth century the right to hereditary renewal of the feudal contract had become an established custom. Frequently the vassal disposed of fiefs he held from his superior lord to other nobles, who thereby became his own vassals. Through this process, known as "subinfeudation," a complicated system of overlordship and vassalage arose, which divided the nobility into various grades according to the size and origin of their fiefs. At the top ranked the holders of great royal fiefs, which in many cases became virtually independent principalities, headed by dukes and counts, who had many vassals of their own. The bottom of the aristocratic hierarchy was formed by those vassals who held only enough land to enable them to serve as mounted knights in the feudal armies.

Like the nobility, the medieval clergy was a distinguished and powerful estate with special legal privileges and carefully guarded prerogatives. The clergy constituted a firmly organized, well-ordered segment of society arranged in a definite hierarchy. The administrative organization of the church resembled a state within the state; in fact, it was a superstate whose jurisdiction extended over every kingdom in Christendom. The medieval church was a temporal as well as a spiritual power: its ruler was the Pope; its provincial governors were archbishops and bishops; it had its own legislative assemblies in synods and councils; it made its own laws and possessed its own courts of law and its own prisons.[12]

Like the secular government, the organization of the medieval clergy was largely based upon landownership. The rural parish priest, at the bottom of the clerical hierarchy, was a resident tenant on the manorial estates whose church he served and was provided a parish house and plot of land by the lord of the manor. The higher prelates, however, the abbots, bishops, archbishops, and the Pope himself, were great landlords in their own right, who controlled thousands of manors, granted fiefs, ruled vassals, governed serfs, and exercised the same temporal powers as the secular feudal lords. Eventually the higher ranks of the ecclesiastical hierarchy came to resemble that of the secular feudal world to the point where the ecclesiastical prestige of the bishops was largely measured by their status as territorial lords.

Under these circumstances it is hardly surprising that the

higher and lower ranks of the clerical hierarchy were sharply divided; the higher clerical offices were increasingly preempted by the younger sons of noble families until the upper ranks of the church hierarchy became almost closed to any but those of noble blood, while the parish priests were generally of servile origin. But despite this feudalization of the medieval church, the clergy never became a closed estate because celibacy prevented its closure. Its members had to be recruited from the other strata of society and notwithstanding the usurpation of higher clerical positions by members of the nobility, the church preserved a measure of opportunity for men of talent and energy whatever their social origins.[13]

Before the rise of towns the large mass of the common people, who formed the basis of the medieval social hierarchy, were peasants who lived on the manorial estates of feudal landlords. They were tenants in various degrees of dependence and bondage. All manorial tenants were required to render labor services on the lord's own holdings (demesne-lands) and in addition had to pay various dues to the lord, usually in kind. In return, each tenant was assigned a hut and a portion of arable land to cultivate as his own. Moreover, tenants had the right to use the common pasture, the woodland, and the wastelands which surrounded the cultivated soil.

Originally there existed various gradations in legal and social status among the tenants. Some were *freemen* who had once owned their holdings outright but had voluntarily placed themselves under the protection of the lord (self-commendation). Although they remained personally free, their liberty was effectively curtailed by the many services, including military duty, and by the dues which the lord levied on their holdings in return for his protection. Most tenants, however, were *villeins* of a semifree status. They were bound to the soil, and if the estate changed hands, they remained with the land and became tenants of the new lord. Finally, some tenants were personal *serfs,* chattels whose very persons belonged to the lord—the social descendants of the rural slaves who had been employed in large numbers on the landed estates of antiquity. But in the closed economy of the self-sufficient medieval manor, which did not produce for a market, the constant supervision and maintenance of unwilling slaves proved cumbersome and inefficient. It was more profitable to attach the serfs to the soil as dependent peasants and treat them like half-free villeins who would support themselves and, at the same time, be held in order by their dominant interest in landholdings. Thus the number of slaves decreased rapidly on the manorial estates and slavery gradually died out in medieval Europe.[14]

The original social distinctions of the rural tenants eventually became blurred and they ultimately blended into one broad stratum of servile peasants, all of whom were tied by heredity to the land they cultivated. They could not leave the land without the consent of the lord, but they could not be sold apart from it or otherwise dispossessed. Their lives were therefore confined to the village or manor on which they lived. They were subject to the manorial courts of justice, presided over by the lord or his bailiff, who rendered judgments according to the custom of the manor. The various dues and services required by the lord often were hard and onerous, but in return the villeins and serfs were exempted from military service and were entitled to protection and shelter from the disturbances of war and external violence. Politically, however, the peasants had no official voice and socially, of course, they were looked down upon by the nobility and the clergy.

By the twelfth century the appearance of a new social stratum began to change the profile of the medieval social order: the bourgeoisie, the merchants and artisans of the nascent medieval towns. The latter were not merely the successors of the Roman and Grecian cities of antiquity, some of which had persisted as seats of bishops and centers of diocesan administration, but had lost most of their urban characteristics as their merchants and artisans had vanished. In fact, most of the medieval towns were entirely new urban centers, founded as speculative ventures by princes and other nobles who wished to acquire dependents who could be taxed in money. Therefore they established markets and towns, protected by walls and fortifications, and populated by wandering merchants and artisans who reappeared on the continent with the revival of commerce and navigation.

The burgesses of the commercial towns that sprang up all over Europe in this period developed a new way of life contrasting sharply with the feudal society which continued outside their walls. Deriving their sustenance not from the cultivation of the soil but from industry and trade the burgesses needed liberty to come and go, as well as other important rights not enjoyed by rural serfs. They obtained (and paid for) charters granting personal freedom and exemption from feudal dues and labor services to all inhabitants of the town and giving them jursidictional and administrative autonomy to organize their community in a way that facilitated their economic activities. "Freedom became the legal status of the bourgeoisie, so much so that it was no longer a personal privilege only, but a territorial one, inherent in urban soil just as serfdom was inherent in manorial soil." [15] Regardless of social origin, men became legally free after having resided for a year and a day within the walls of a town, a fact which opened up an avenue of escape for rural serfs who desired to flee from the authority of their lord.

The inhabitants of the medieval towns came to occupy so important a place as a separate stratum in the social order that they were recognized as a "third estate." Like the nobility and the clergy, the bourgeoisie had a separate legal status which set them off from the rural masses as a privileged class. As the towns grew wealthier they acquired considerable political power and their inhabitants gained social prestige. Each town formed a separate political entity which jealously guarded its prerogatives and privileges, many towns coming to dominate extensive rural subject territories which they ruled and administered much in the manner of the feudal lords and princes.

The townsmen, however, hardly constituted a socially homogeneous body. Like the other medieval social strata they were internally differentiated into segments which differed sharply in wealth, prestige, and political power. There arose a more or less distinct cleavage between three urban classes: an upper class of wealthy merchants, who from the beginning monopolized the town government and formed an urban patriciate; a middle class of smaller retailers and master craftsmen; and a growing laboring class of propertyless men, who worked as wage earners or journeymen for the merchants and master craftsmen. To be sure, in many towns, though not in all, the merchant oligarchy was eventually overthrown by the craft guilds that achieved political domination. But this did not result in political democracy or social and economic equality. Rather the merchant elite was replaced by an elite of master craftsmen who soon constituted themselves into a privileged ruling class until they, in turn, found themselves pushed aside, centuries later, by a new class of manufacturers and industrial entrepreneurs.

Although dominated by a privileged minority, the urban social order nevertheless differed fundamentally from the feudal social hierarchy which continued to govern the surrounding rural areas until long after the end of the Middle Ages. The urban social system from the beginning was a *class system,* founded on monetary wealth and occupation, not an estate system depending on hereditary relationships to landholdings. Despite sharp cleavages and conflicts between the urban classes and the attempts of the town patricians to protect their privileged position through aristocratic exclusiveness, the barriers which separated the simple journeyman or poor urban wage earner from the wealthy merchants were never as insuperable as the wall which divided the feudal noble from the rural serf. The urban barriers were essentially economic and could be hurdled by monetary acquisition and financial success.

The way of life of the medieval townsmen and their social hierarchy represent the first manifestations of the modern class system which eventually became a characteristic feature of all Western societies. But the way in which the class system displaced and superseded the estate system of social stratification was a long-drawn-out process which was not completed in most European countries until the first half of the nineteenth century.

One aspect of this extended process is the fact that the urban population remained very limited in size. Despite their increasing social influence the townsmen never comprised more than a tenth of the total population of any Western country until the industrial revolution. Thus the bulk of the people remained rural, and despite changes in the agricultural system—for example, the peasants were gradually permitted to commute dues and services into money rents, and the serfs eventually became free tenant farmers—the nobility remained a legally privileged estate, retaining its position at the apex of the social hierarchy. The aristocratic style of life set the tone, the nobility looking down upon the bourgeoisie, whose wealthiest members often aspired to become ennobled themselves. Thus the vestiges of an antiquated feudal social hierarchy persisted: until the end of the eighteenth century the different estates remained not only socially but also legally distinct in all European countries.

Eventually, however, the owners of the newly arising industries, who had become the leaders of the bourgeoisie, were increasingly restive because of the restrictions by which the aristocratic order hampered the free development of a capitalistic market economy. In the French Revolution, which soon spread throughout European society, the bourgeoisie arose in revolt and asserted itself against nobility, clergy, and royalty. Legal privileges for the older estates were abolished and personal liberty for all as well as equality before the law were established in principle. The revolution completed the transition from the estate to the class system. In its ascent to economic power the bourgeoisie had finally won political power and social prestige, and the order of inherited social estates was replaced by a system of social classes better adapted to the needs of modern urban-industrial societies.

III

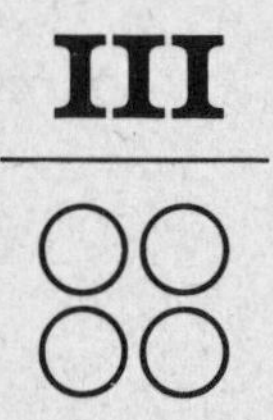

Dimensions of Social Stratification in Modern Society

The brief and necessarily oversimplified account of the development of social stratification presented in the preceding chapter is of more than historical interest. It not only indicates the principal historical forces that shaped and changed the social order from which the modern Western class system emerged, but it also serves to illustrate by comparison some of the conceptual difficulties and dilemmas that the observer faces when he attempts to describe and analyze the nature of our contemporary class structure.

In preceding stratification systems, despite their many concrete differences, the various social strata were set off from each other by fairly clear-cut lines of demarcation. Members of different strata were distinguished not only by differences in income, wealth, and occupation, but also by distinctive styles of life. Each stratum was characterized by patterns of conduct and behavior standards that gave clear recognition to its place in the social hierarchy. Differing sharply in rank, honor, prestige, and political power, the various strata were also separated by severe limits on intermarriage and social intercourse, by a sharp sense of social distance, and by outward symbols of their distinctive ways of life. At the same time, the prevailing ideologies and religious creeds explained and justified the existing hierarchical arrangements. There was thus no difficulty either in recognizing a given individual's social position or in perceiving the system as a whole.

A contrasting situation prevails in modern Western societies, where social classes are not set apart by tangible boundaries. In feudal Europe it was easy enough to distinguish merchants from aristocrats at first sight by their distinctive dress, but one would be hard put to identify the class position of people on the streets of an American city, although this selection might be feasible at the extremes of the class scale. Modern social classes have no legal standing; nor are they organized groups. There are no official, rigid criteria of class position. Upper- and middle-class status symbols are in principle accessible to anyone with the necessary wealth to purchase them. Furthermore, the movement of individuals and families from one class to another is free of legal restrictions. Significantly, the official ideology of democratic societies does not justify class differences, but on the contrary tends to deny them.

Although historical changes have made it more difficult to determine the class membership of particular individuals and even of certain groups, socially significant class differences mark contemporary Western societies. Even in the United States, with its pronounced equalitarian ideology, social class differences are a reality that divides the society and influences the ways of life of its members. In modern societies all people may be considered equal before the law and titles of nobility may have been abolished, but there remain inequalities of income and wealth, of prestige and esteem, of power and authority. Moreover, as in other societies, these are not merely individual inequalities and differentials; a feature of modern society is a graded series of ranks, the members of each rank having similar opportunities to obtain the goods and advantages that are culturally valued.

While in earlier societies the differential distribution of property and income was directly and closely related to differences in rank, honor, and prestige, modern class systems are not characterized by such a close and visible correlation between economic inequality and other social differences. In the highly complex and more loosely integrated industrial society, the prestige, authority, and power of the individual are not necessarily matched by his economic position. This is to say, the interrelationship between economic inequality and the differential distribution of power and prestige is considerably more complicated in modern class systems than it was, for example, in the feudal estate hierarchy.

Of fundamental sociological importance are the several different dimensions in modern systems of stratification. Each of these dimensions constitutes a separate rank order with respect to specific opportunities by which certain values and advantages may be obtained, though the different rank orders are interrelated. Together they account for the wide range of opportunities in modern societies.[1]

CLASS, LIFE CHANCES, AND CLASS CONSCIOUSNESS

A first dimension of social stratification, the *economic,* stratifies modern populations according to amount and source of income, which is usually derived from a set of occupational activities, the ownership of property, or both. Differences in income, property, and occupation divide the members of modern societies into statistically distinguishable strata, or *classes.* Classes are thus aggregates of individuals and families in similar economic positions. Individuals of the same or similar economic position have identical or similar goods and services to offer in the system of production and distribution and therefore receive identical or similar monetary rewards in the marketplace. This also means that in modern industrial societies members of the same economic class have similar chances to obtain certain values and opportunities that are of primary importance for life and survival. "Everything from the chance to stay alive during the first year after birth to the chance to view fine arts, the chance to remain healthy and grow tall, and if sick to get well again quickly, the chance to avoid becoming a juvenile delinquent—and very crucially, the chance to complete an intermediary or higher educational grade" [2]—all these *life chances* are crucially influenced by one's position in the economic class structure.

Note, however, that these classes are usually neither communities nor organized groups but simply aggregates of people possessing similar economic interests. The members of a class may or may not be aware of the likeness of their economic interests and life chances. And even if such awareness does exist, it may influence their behavior in quite different ways. One consequence of the recognition of a shared class situation is class solidarity and *class consciousness.* In this case the members of a given class come to identify like (individualized) interests as common (shared) interests and perhaps to organize in such associations as labor unions and political parties designed in part to pursue these interests, which in turn may lead to open conflict and struggle with people in other class situations. But this development does not necessarily take place. Class awareness and class consciousness may only lead to diffuse reactions. For example, industrial workers over the world may tend to restrict their production by virtue of a more or less tacit agreement, but whether or not they band together and engage in economic and political class action and class warfare depends on a number of circumstances, primarily perhaps on whether the workers consciously recognize the causal connections between their life chances and the structure of the economic order that determines them. Concerted action also depends on the availability of an articulate leadership and the physical possibilities of organizing and acting in unison. Often one or all of these factors are lacking, and there may be many additional reasons that prevent the rise of class consciousness and class action despite the factual existence of sharp class differentials in the distribution of income and property.

Whether or not class consciousness and class action arise from a given class situation is always a matter to be determined by study of concrete cases. In Chapter VII we shall return to this question with specific reference to the United States.

STATUS AND STATUS GROUPS

A second dimension of stratification in modern societies is the *status* order. The term *status* as used in this study refers to the differentiation of prestige and deference among individuals and groups in a society.

Prestige rests upon interpersonal recognition, always involving at least one individual who claims deference and another who honors the claim. A person's claim to prestige and his place in the prestige hierarchy generally depend upon the way in which his social positions and behavior are evaluated by the members of his community. Individuals who occupy a similar position in the status hierarchy of a community tend to form *status groups;* that is, they treat each other as social equals, encouraging the intermarriage of their children, joining the same clubs and associations, and participating together in such informal activities as visiting, dances, dinners, and receptions. However, some status hierarchies may also be nationwide or even international, involving, for example, a person's status as a statesman, a film actor, a sports hero, or a scientist. In fact, there are as many status hierarchies as there are distinguishable patterns of interpersonal relations.[3]

Of paramount sociological importance is the realization that in modern societies the economic order and the status order are closely related but not identical; therefore classes and status groups must be carefully distinguished. Although the two dimensions are distinct, the status order is to a high degree conditioned by the class structure and in its turn reacts upon it. The reason for this relationship lies in the fact that since economic factors necessarily play a primary role in industrial societies, people maintain intimate social relations largely with others in similar economic positions. Social intercourse, intermarriage, and participation in clubs and other organizations tend to be restricted to others in one's own economic bracket. A close correspondence is therefore often found between class position and rank in the status hierarchy, with wealthy people generally possessing high prestige. But no exact correspondence and, in fact, frequent discrepancies exist between an individual's class position and his standing in the prestige hierarchy. Such discrepancies cannot be explained in static terms but should be understood dynamically as the result of an individual's mobility along only some of the stratification dimensions or as a consequence of an established social distinction between the class and status hierarchies as a whole.

A status group can be characterized by specific behavior patterns, a definite "style of life," which must be adhered to by those who wish to belong to it. Linked with this expectation are tendencies toward closure, as manifested in restrictions on intermarriage and social participation of those who "don't act right" and therefore do not belong. When restrictions of this kind result in complete group endogamy and full closure, status groups take on castelike features. But in modern societies this development is confined for the most part to differences that are defined as "ethnic" or "racial."

In general, the effect of status hierarchies seems to be the stabilization of the existing class structure, their principal function in this respect being the legitimation of class positions. Thus groups that have attained high economic positions usually attempt to solidify these positions by restricting status recognition and excluding others from access to the status symbols which they try to monopolize.[4] The result is that while high status is dependent in the long run upon high class position—the maintenance of a prestigious style of life costs money—there is no necessary correspondence between them at any given time. A fishmonger, for example, who has acquired wealth through skillful operations in the impersonal market may not be accepted as a social equal without reservations by the "blue bloods" of Boston's Beacon Hill or Philadelphia's Main Line, however faithfully he imitates their style of life. But they may accept his descendants who have been educated in the conventions of their status groups and who have not dirtied their own hands by manual labor. And the reverse also holds; impoverished descendants of old Southern plantation families, for instance, may retain their high-status reputation for several generations after their wealth has been lost and receive more deference from more people than well-to-do newcomers who lack the appropriate grandparents. In the long run, however, the style of life required by high status necessarily depends upon commensurate class position, and in the course of time the broken-down aristocrat becomes simply broken-down and the son of the nouveau-riche fishmonger becomes a man of "clean, old wealth." [5]

The interrelations between the dimensions of class and status are thus dynamic, reciprocal, and in constant flux. Status groups tend to grow strong and to hinder and retard the operations of sheer economic forces when economic conditions are relatively stable. By the same token, significant economic changes tend to weaken status restrictions and may even break down existing prestige distinctions altogether. An illuminating example of the operation of cross-pressures between class and status systems in American society can be seen in the use of restrictive covenants by which established prestigious groups sometimes attempt to keep out "undesirable elements" who have risen in the class structure to the point where they can afford to purchase high-status symbols in the form of property in the best residential areas. In this context class mobility is defined as a threat to the privileged positions and stability of the high-status groups, who wield the restrictive covenant as a defensive weapon. Where dominant groups are successful in keeping out the "nouveaux riches," these newcomers often form parallel status hierarchies, developing their own exclusive residential sections and organizing their own Junior Leagues, country clubs, and resorts.

POWER

A third dimension of social stratifications is the *power* structure. We have defined power as the ability to control the behavior of others. Sociologically, power refers especially to the control that certain groups and individuals are able to exercise over the life chances of others.

The unequal distribution of power in modern society is linked with both the class and the status hierarchies, the connection between economic position and the ability to exercise power being especially close. Entrepreneurial and property-owning upper classes obviously hold great power over job markets, their investment decisions and market operations affecting the life chances of large numbers of others. But in urban-industrial societies such immense power rarely goes unchallenged. The propertyless wage earners may organize labor unions and farmers may band together in associations in an effort to offset the industrialists' power by the exercise of countervailing power.[6]

In the maneuvering and struggle that ensue different classes and interest groups often seek to transform economic power into political power in order to influence or determine the policies or activities of the state. This is accomplished directly through political parties, which may represent the interests of a specific class, a typical situation in many European countries, or indirectly through the activities of organized pressure groups and lobbies, a common device in the United States. It should be noted, however, that ability to wield economic and political power is not identical with its actual exercise. Whether or not a given class or interest group transforms its potential power into actual power depends upon a number of factors, including the objective conditions and opportunities, the will and purpose, and finally the skill and judgment of its leaders.[7]

A close connection also exists between power and prestige. The very fact that individuals or groups hold positions in which they can make important decisions that affect the lives of others generally brings the power-holders a good deal of prestige. This obviously applies to those who hold key economic positions, but prestige is not confined to the economically powerful. A large amount of power and influence is today also exercised by those who head other large-scale hierarchical organizations, such as the government, the armed forces, the major universities, the labor unions, and the church. These are organizations of varying prestige in modern society. A successful military or political career often bestows both power and prestige upon an individual, which he can then "cash in" for a high economic position if he so desires. Retired generals and heads of government agencies, though not labor leaders as a rule, thus find open doors to the top levels of the corporate business hierarchy.

The relationship between the distribution of power, class structure, and status hierarchy is then highly dynamic. In stable periods most people occupy quite similar positions in all three hierarchies, and the three dimensions overlap closely. But when social change is rapid because of technological or economic shifts or war, this correlation is disturbed and numerous discrepancies occur. A whole class may rise at the expense of another, established status groups may be challenged by new groups who have suddenly acquired wealth and power, and many individuals may find that they have moved along the different dimensions of stratification at unequal rates of speed.

SOCIAL MOBILITY

This brings us, finally, to a fourth concept of fundamental importance in the analysis of modern social stratification, *social mobility*. Social mobility refers to the movement of individuals up and down the class, status, and power hierarchies.

We pointed out in Chapter I that the frequency and extent to which individuals move between social strata are among the crucial criteria used to distinguish the major types of stratification systems: caste, estate, and class. To be sure, some mobility up and down the social ladder exists in every society, including India where, notwithstanding the rigid caste system, whole castes and subcastes, as well as some individuals, rise and fall in the rank hierarchy. As we have seen, social mobility also exists in estate systems, but there it is rigidly circumscribed and limited and usually involves a change in legal status. Only in modern class systems, where formal and legal barriers are absent and where equality of opportunity is an officially acknowledged ideal, is social mobility viewed as commonplace and normal.

According to democratic ideology a person's social position should depend solely upon his own qualities and achievements and he should be free to rise above or fall below his parents' class and status groups in accordance with his personal capacities. Correspondingly, social classes should consist merely of temporary aggregates of individuals who happen to have achieved similar social positions at any particular time. In reality, of course, modern class systems deviate considerably from these ideals. The extent to which it is actually possible for individuals to move between classes and status groups is a matter of empirical study in each concrete case.

The foregoing discussion and definition of the concepts of class, life chances, status group, power, class consciousness, and social mobility have provided us with necessary tools which we shall employ in the chapters that follow. There our task will be to describe and to analyze the class structure of contemporary American society.

A MODEL OF THE PERPETUATION OF CLASSES

Although dimensions of stratification have some degree of independence of one another as bases for describing and analyzing the major kinds of hierarchies in industrial societies, they are also causally interrelated. These interrelations are very important and can best be shown in terms of a theoretical framework designed to organize the dynamic flow of social forces that suggest both how a stratification system perpetuates itself and how it may change. We may think of this framework as a model of the operation of society over the generations viewed in terms of typical individuals born into a particular class and living out their lives within the flux of class structures and forces until they themselves give birth to the next generation of societal members who in turn assume a similar class position.

This life-cycle model of the perpetuation of social classes makes use of four interlinked categories of any social system (see Figure 2). In its barest outlines the model simply states the following: The typical adult members of different classes hold *differential positions in the social, especially economic, organization of the society*. This creates and perpetuates *interaction differentials* such that class members tend to be segregated and to live and interrelate with one another within similar life experiences. In turn differential *class subcultures* with distinct features tend to develop. The *new generation* of children born into such subcultures is socialized and educated in differential ways. Again, this is due especially to the *interaction differentials* fostered by the subcultural and sometimes legal situations. Such differential socialization and education shape class *differentials in personality traits and acquired skills,* which, to the extent that they are relevant to the qualifications necessary for recruitment into adult social positions in the society, lead back to the category of differential positions in the social organization and hence to the perpetuation of social class or caste positions. Thus we have a feedback flow of events from generation to generation, similar to what Gunnar Myrdal, in his classic study of the American Negro, called the "vicious circle" of anti-Negro discrimination.[8] The latter situation may in fact be viewed as a special case of the more general process of social class perpetuation.

Such a model can only be highly schematic and cannot therefore do justice to the richness of detail found in different his-

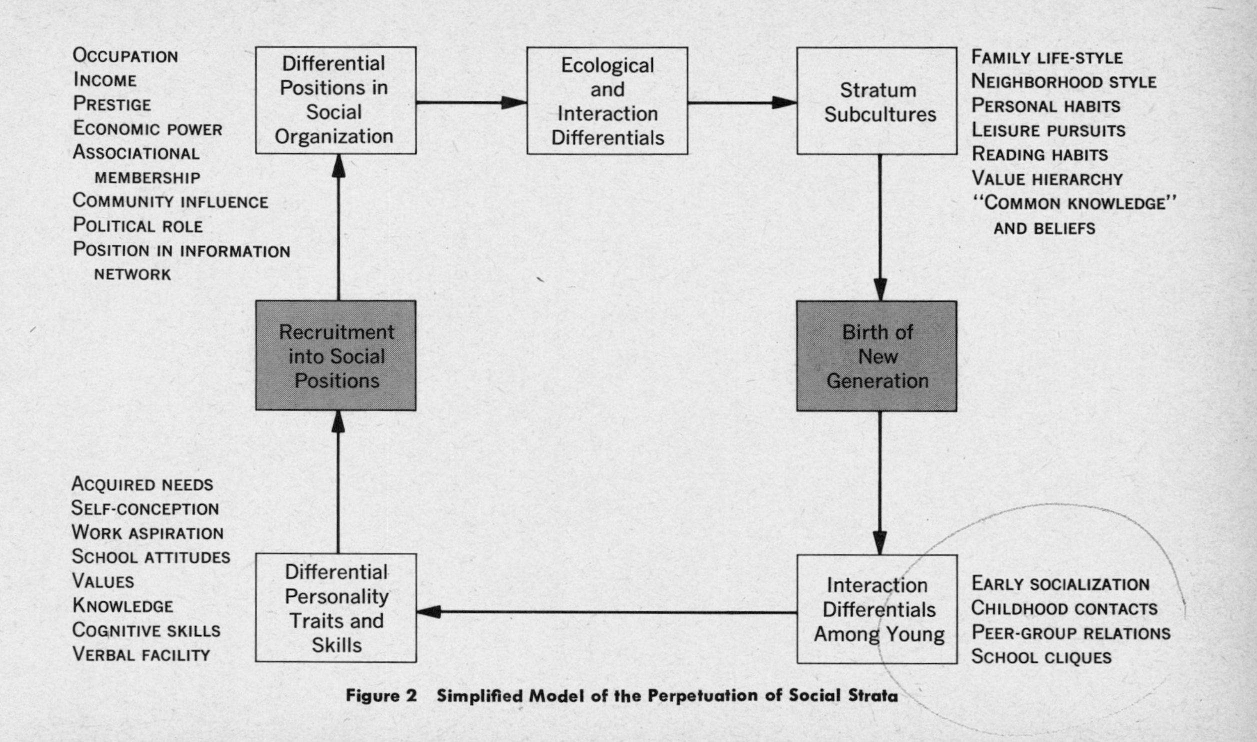

Figure 2 Simplified Model of the Perpetuation of Social Strata

torical societies. For most premodern societies our model would thus have to insert a place for the strict legal rules, the sumptuary legislation, or the religious dogmas and customs that reinforce the social and psychological mechanisms of the model and serve to maintain a very rigid perpetuation of class or caste over the generations. In modern societies these institutional forms are absent or less restrictive, and most of the perpetuation is due primarily to the social, economic, and psychological mechanisms described in the model.

Moreover, such a schematic model implies a simple causal flow from one category to the next, when in fact each of the categories is directly or indirectly related to each of the others and in a mutually reciprocal way. The causal flow of the chart also implies a simple time sequence from one category to the next, but in reality each category makes its effects felt continuously (although there is no doubt that each is especially acute at certain points of the life cycle).

Let us examine the model more closely as it applies to the modern case of social classes. We may start (quite arbitrarily) at the upper-left box, which represents the point in the life cycle at which adults are filling their *differential positions in the social organization* of society. (The factors listed alongside each box represent some of the more important variables that research shows to be closely related to class differences.)[9] This means, first and foremost in industrial society, that individuals are performing different occupations to which their income, prestige, and the amount of economic and political power or authority they may wield are closely tied. In turn, these occupations have the effect of segregating groupings of individuals differentially into neighborhoods, mutual interaction networks, and common-experience groupings. Membership and leadership in voluntary associations come to reflect occupational class, with very little participation and almost no leadership from the lowest groups. Political position and activity show a class bias, with the lowest status groups playing a minimal political role and community power and influence tending to concentrate in the upper and middle groups. Many community-power studies give a picture of the higher classes showing a greater degree of participation and involvement in the community and thus a tendency to dominate its political, economic, and other organizational activities, as well as its intellectual life and its leadership. The lower classes, on the other hand, show a much lesser degree of concern with and knowledge about the affairs and decision-making arrangements of the larger community. This lack of involvement and knowledge of affairs extends to the single mechanism by which the majority of persons can easily participate in policy decisions affecting their total lives and environment, namely, the democratic vote. Here, studies such as those of Angus Campbell and his colleagues provide a portrait of the average American voter as politically ignorant, his thinking impoverished and unstructured ideologically, confused about party policies and their implications, and quite unable to judge government actions, appraise its goals, or evaluate the means used to pursue them.[10]

Such circumstances, then, with their segregating and limiting effects—physically, psychologically, and socially—lead to the development or perpetuation of *class subcultures,* the second of our major analytical categories. We here use the concept of subculture to refer to a complex of interrelated learned beliefs, attitudes, values, and patterns of behavior common to a grouping within the larger society. These traits become generalized in symbols and thoughtways forming an ethos that reflects and is reflected by the details of group life. Most important, such traits are seized upon by other subgroups as bases for perceiving and acting toward members of the subculture, as determining their standing in the community, or as a means to "hang people on their own peg." Some of the many class differences in subcultural "life-style" recorded by research include differences in respect to type of residence, leisure and recreation, family life and ritual, church preference, sex mores and behavior, fashions, musical taste, drinking habits, and types of deviant behavior.

How does the new generation, born into a segregated or partially segregated class subculture, with parents holding certain social positions, come to reflect those class differentials, grow up to become adults similar in important ways to their parents, and assume in turn similar social and subcultural positions? One important process at work here is that of *differential social interaction.* In all major phases of the younger years the class subculture restricts the individuals, groups, and environmental situations with which one interacts, thus biasing his psychological, social, and sometimes physical development. Substantial research documents this process, showing its impact upon many aspects of infant socialization, childhood contacts at play and in early schooling, and the growth of peer-group relations and high school and college cliques and dating patterns. Studies indicate that this impact is not just a passive result of neighborhood ecological patterns but is often actively promoted by parents. Several investigations have brought out the way in which middle-class parents take action to see to it that their children belong to certain organizations—such as the Boy Scouts or church groups—that teach or uphold middle-class ways of life, and control informal play situations so as to keep their children in the company of others who have "correct" manners, language, and attitudes. This process, often aided by teachers and by other members of the child's primary groups, continues through youth and early adulthood. As the child becomes older it becomes socially and psychologically more "comfortable" for him to remain in familiar surroundings and social situations, so that his own selective preferences come to reinforce those of his primary groups.

The net results of these selective pressures on the various classes of young people is to inculcate in them *differential personality traits, skills, and abilities.* The network of primary relationships within which social interaction and communication occur has the direct effect of shaping the human mind and capabilities, of determining attitudes, organizing actions, supporting norms, and establishing a more or less unique world view. Research has documented the class-based character of one's self-conception, acquired needs, occupational aspirations and expectations, attitudes toward school and the learning of skills, and the development of a wide range of political, economic, religious, and other values and attitudes. Studies have also brought out the class differentials in the more cognitive aspects of the psyche, such as the quantity and quality of knowledge, ability to score high on "intelligence" tests, and problem-solving techniques. In sum, by the time one has become a young adult, social class has acted as an important factor in helping to shape the various qualifications and skills with which the individual will face the problem of entering into an occupation and assuming other positions in the larger social structure. Depending on the degree of rigidity of the stratification system, the young individual tends to enter into occupations and other social positions that are more or less similar to those of his parents. We have thus returned to our starting point in the cycle, from which we may follow this next generation of societal members, who will tend to continue to interact within their own class milieu, marry within it, and establish a home in the "appropriate" neighborhood, perpetuate the class subculture, and in turn give birth to a new generation of class exemplaries.

As we have pointed out, this is a highly schematic model. It assumes a fairly stable society and fits most accurately the relatively rigid or "closed" societies of the past. Within limits, nevertheless, the model is useful in the study of modern industrial societies, for they are still marked by a significant degree of stratification despite their greater fluidity, fairly high degree of mobility between classes, and consequent lack of sharp class lines.

As suggested above, this model may also be used as a baseline from which to indicate the mechanisms by which individuals may, at one point or another along the "vicious circle," leave one class level and enter another. Here we merely outline some of the more important of these mechanisms. With respect to *differential positions in the social organization,* especially in modern societies, individuals are of course not necessarily fixed in ascribed social positions but may engage in career mobility, moving into occupational positions that are higher in income, prestige, or power than those of their parents. A very important factor associated with such mobility is the fact that the occupational structure—or the *opportunity structure,* as it has been called—of modern industrial societies changes quite rapidly, so that more positions at higher levels are created and made available. Thus, as societies continue to develop industrially, the number of skilled, white-collar, semiprofessional, and professional jobs increases, while rural and unskilled occupations decrease. This structural change accounts, then, for a substantial amount of the mobility of young people into higher-level positions than those of their parents; it also explains a good part of the career mobility of adults who leave lower-ranked occupations for higher ones.

Some shift in the distribution of classes has also come about in modern societies by way of the democratic vote. The latter has meant an increment in the ability of citizens to influence community, state, and national decisions, resulting at times in some change in the control of social and economic resources and hence in the distribution of social products, transfer payments, and the like. This political process and its effects are a large and important area that we can only mention here.

We have seen that the individual's position in the social structure is related to a number of ecological and interactional constraints that channel the attitudes, beliefs, and values which make up *class subcultures.* These constraints, however, are not fully effective, and many individuals and families engage in social relations that help to inculcate beliefs and values that are not typical of their objective social class. This situation may be especially important as an environing influence on a growing number of children in modern industrial societies and thus changes their life chances.

In earlier, agrarian societies, in which communities were relatively isolated from one another and there were no mass media of communication and little intermingling of populations, subcultures tended to be fairly clear-cut, with little interaction between them. In urban, industrialized societies, however, with well-developed mass media and close proximity and high visibility of subgroups of different classes, isolation is broken down, not all neighborhoods are single-class, leisure pursuits and personal habits tend to cross class lines, and beliefs, attitudes, and values are only partly shaped by class subculture. Thus, despite the fact that there are significant class subcultural differences in modern societies, there are also large numbers of marginal individuals and families and hence a lack of sharp subcultural groupings on a purely class basis. This situation means, as we have said, that individuals newly born into society may be subject to subcultural advantages or disadvantages which are not consonant with the objective class positions of their parents as measured by income or occupation.

Similar considerations apply to *interactional differentials* among the young. Although data on modern societies show that early socialization, childhood interactions, and school cliques occur on a class basis to a significant degree, there are wide opportunities for cross-class interactions. Substantial numbers of the young consequently transcend their ascribed class with respect to attitudes, values, and beliefs. This "inconsistency" is especially important to the degree that lower-class young persons learn to aspire to and strive for middle- or upper-class occupational positions. Perhaps the single most important factor allowing persons to break out of the class cycle is educational opportunity, which provides *cognitive and other skills* required for social mobility. Although the amount and kind of education are highly correlated with class level of parents, a significant number of the young are able and willing, for reasons suggested above, to attain levels of education that permit them to qualify for occupational positions above the class level of the parents.

Finally, all of the above considerations mean that, in the recruitment of persons into differential positions in the larger organization of society, many individuals of lower- or higher-class origin attain positions consonant with a different social class. This pattern means that there is a substantial amount of upward mobility, though most of it is of fairly small degree, as well as a fairly large amount of downward mobility (a pattern to be examined in Chapter VIII). We have thus returned to our initial point of departure in the theoretical model of social-class perpetuation, having noted some of the more important mechanisms by which the individuals in modern societies may break out of the "vicious circle." This theme recurs frequently in the following chapters.

IV

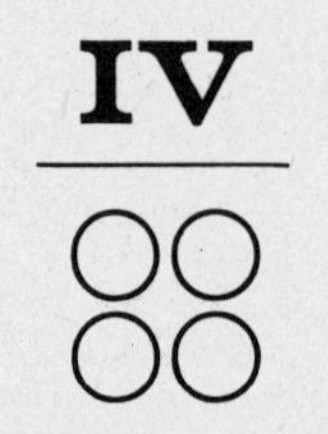

Class in American Society: The Distribution of Life Chances

Casual observers and temporary visitors from abroad are often impressed by the many differences that distinguish the American class structure from European systems of social stratification. To a large extent these differences are the result of divergent historical experiences of the nations on the two sides of the Atlantic. Although classes have now generally superseded traditional estates throughout Western society, the stratification systems of most European countries still exhibit vestiges of the old estate order. England, with its hereditary nobility, its system of dual education, and the marked social distance between "gentlemen" and "the lower orders" (though the situation is changing today), provides a good example of the blending of older estate features with a modern class structure. In other European countries, too, class divisions are quite obvious and taken for granted.

The absence of a feudal past, the lack of a hereditary aristocracy, accounts in large part for the different development that stratification has taken in the United States. From the beginning, social life on this continent was new and relatively unburdened with the traditions of hereditary status and fixed prerogatives. Here the "common man" was not expected to "know his place" and to show deference to "his betters" as he was in Europe. Once the United States had been founded and British rule overcome, fewer vested political and economic interests existed than in Europe. Thus the new United States soon became the goal of millions of individuals, many of whom sought to escape traditional social inequalities. In ever-increasing numbers they streamed across the ocean, lured by the promise of freedom and equal opportunity for all.

Ideological equalitarianism, together with the rapid social change and economic growth made possible by the exploitation of abundant natural resources, account for the less rigid, more dynamic class structure that has arisen in the United States. As we have noted earlier, so strong is the ideal of equal opportunity in this country that a definite tendency has existed—and persists in some measure—to deny class differences and to consider success as solely the result of individual effort and merit. "Anyone who has it in him can get to the top in the United States" is a traditional cliché still proclaimed at the family dinner table, in Fourth of July orations, and in the "public relations" advertisements of business corporations.

As in the case of most social ideals, however, the idea of equality of opportunity is only imperfectly embodied in American practice. Large segments of the population, for example, are denied equal access to opportunity on the basis of skin color, religion, or "nationality." If the absence of estatelike characteristics makes the American class system unique, it is likewise true that the intrusion of racial castelike features is almost without parallel in modern Western experience. In fact, the coexistence of a strongly equalitarian ideology and a racial "caste" system represents one of the puzzling paradoxes of American society and is responsible for some of our gravest social problems.

Quite apart from this caste phenomenon (to which we shall return in Chapter V), equality of opportunity does not exist for a large proportion of individuals in the United States. A boy born into the family of a business executive, who is sent to a good school, attends a well-known college, and is given a stake when he starts his career, obviously has a much better chance "to get ahead" than the son of an unskilled laborer or of a tenant farmer. Inherited position, wealth, social "connections," formal education, and other advantages unrelated to personal qualities and achievements play a major role in determining the life chances of individuals in American society. Some of the effects of such distinctions can be documented by statistical data, which demonstrate the existence of sharp differentials in the distribution of scarce values in this country.

DIFFERENCES IN INCOME, WEALTH, AND OCCUPATION

We shall discuss in this section three important measures of economic inequality: the distribution of money income among families, the distribution of amount of wealth held as various kinds of assets, and the relative shares of the total national income received by income deciles. Let us begin our investigation of life chances by examining the distribution of total money income among the more than fifty million families and individuals living alone who constitute the income-receiving segment of our population. Table I shows that in 1962 the median income was $5,308; that is, one-half of all families and individuals received more and one-half received less than this amount. It should be stressed, however, that this table lists family income. The incomes of individuals are, of course, much lower. Thus in 1959

TABLE I Percentage Distribution of Total Money Incomes of Families and Unrelated Individuals (1962)

Total Money Income	Families and Unrelated Individuals	
	Percent of 100.0	*Cumulative Percentage*
Less than $500	3.6%	3.6%
$500–$999	4.9	8.5
$1,000–$1,499	5.8	14.3
$1,500–$1,999	4.9	19.2
$2,000–$2,499	4.8	24.0
$2,500–$2,999	4.2	28.2
$3,000–$3,499	4.7	32.9
$3,500–$3,999	4.4	37.3
$4,000–$4,499	4.7	42.0
$4,500–$4,999	4.7	46.7
$5,000–$5,999	10.7	57.4
$6,000–$6,999	9.5	66.9
$7,000–$7,999	7.6	74.5
$8,000–$9,999	10.5	85.0
$10,000–$14,999	10.8	95.8
$15,000–$24,999	3.4	99.2
$25,000 and over	.8	100.0

Median income = $5,308

SOURCE: Compiled from *Current Population Reports,* Series P–60, No. 41 (October 1963), Table 12, p. 35.

the median income of persons fourteen years old and over *who had income* was $2,800. It is clear that many families have multiple earners.

Further inspection of the table shows that the distribution of income was quite unequal: 4.2 percent had incomes above $15,000. The incomes of 37 percent, or more than one-third of all families and individuals, were less than $4,000. It does not take much imagination to visualize the very different types of living that can be bought by families at these widely varying income levels. The differences in total life chances between the top 4 percent and the bottom 24 percent in terms of food, shelter, clothing, health, education, recreation, and general comfort are very wide indeed. Even the differences between the top 33 percent, whose incomes ranged above $7,000, and the other 67 percent suggest considerable inequalities of opportunity.

TABLE II Major Occupation Groups of the Employed Labor Force (1962)

Occupation	Percent Employed	
	White	*Nonwhite*
White Collar		
Professional, technical, and kindred workers	12.6%	5.3%
Proprietors, managers, and officials	11.9	2.6
Clerical, sales, and kindred workers	22.8	8.8
Manual		
Craftsmen, foremen, and kindred workers	13.6	6.0
Operatives and kindred workers	17.5	19.9
Service workers, including private household	10.6	32.8
Laborers	4.3	13.6
Farm		
Farmers and farm managers	4.0	2.7
Farm laborers	2.8	8.3
Total percent	100.0	100.0

SOURCE: U.S. Bureau of the Census, *Statistical Abstract of the United States: 1963* (Washington, D.C.: Government Printing Office, 1963), Table 304, p. 231.

Since occupation rather than the ownership of property is the main source of income for the overwhelming majority of the population in the United States, in discussing differential life chances we should consider the occupational structure. As Table II shows, of the white employed labor force in 1962, about half were manual workers, with 32 percent holding semi-skilled and unskilled jobs and 14 percent holding skilled manual jobs. Another 47 percent were engaged in white-collar occupations: 23 percent held clerical and sales jobs, 12 percent were business proprietors, managers, and officials, and over 12 percent were professional and semiprofessional people. Finally, about 7 percent were farmers and farm laborers. To be noted is the marked difference in occupational distribution for the nonwhite segment of the population.

In our modern industrial society, where most economic production is for the market, there necessarily exists a close connection between occupational structure and income distribution. Only a small number of Americans derive a significant proportion of their income from the ownership of property and its yields; for the vast majority the amount of income received depends primarily upon the job. A man's opportunities to produce and to sell goods or services in the market therefore largely determine his chances to obtain the countless things that money can buy in a pecuniary society.

TABLE III Distribution of Total Money Income by Occupation of Family Head (1962)

Occupation of Family Head	*Median Income*
Self-employed, professional, and technical workers	$13,940
Salaried managers, officials, and proprietors	9,437
Salaried professional and technical workers	9,077
Craftsmen, foremen, and kindred workers	7,571
Sales workers	7,686
Self-employed managers, officials, and proprietors	6,980
Clerical and kindred workers	6,806
Operatives and kindred workers	6,412
Service workers, except private household	5,663
Laborers	5,351
Farmers and farm managers	3,596
Farm laborers	3,457

SOURCE: *Current Population Reports,* Series P–60, No. 40 (June 26, 1963), Table 3, p. 3.

As Table III indicates, people engaged in farming and nonskilled manual workers, who together make up almost one-half of our total labor force, are at the bottom of the income scale. At the top rank are the professionals and the salaried business managers, officials, and proprietors, occupations that constitute about one-tenth of the labor force. Between these two groupings are the broad ranks of clerical and sales workers, self-employed businessmen, and skilled manual craftsmen and foremen (whose median incomes nowadays often exceed those of small business enterprisers and clerical white-collar workers). Of course, these broad occupational categories include wide variations of individual incomes, but Table III provides a reasonably accurate general picture of the relationship between income differentials and occupational structure.

Though the distribution of income shows up a fair amount of inequality, greater extremes can be seen in the distribution of wealth. People in the higher income ranges, of course, hold the bulk of the wealth. Thus in 1960, of those in the lowest income tenth 36 percent held no assets and about 15 percent held assets worth over $10,000; while practically all of those in the highest tenth held assets, 71 percent held assets worth over $10,000, and 41 percent had total assets of over $25,000.[1] With respect to particular types of assets, estimates show that about 6 percent of the people hold all the assets in unincorporated business, 17 percent hold all the real estate assets (other than equity in home), and 14 percent own all the privately held corporate stock.[2] But within these small percentages the concentration is even greater (see Table IV). In fact, a study of the top wealth-holders of 1953, who made up 1 percent of the total population (or 1.6 percent of adults), found that this group held 32 percent of the total personal wealth of the country, 82 percent of all stock in the personal sector, 38 percent of United States government bonds, and 100 percent of state and local bonds.[3]

The great bulk of this wealth, as well as of annual income, derives not from salaries earned while performing an occupation or profession but from the institutionalized property arrangements characteristic of Western capitalist society. And it is important to recognize that, viewing the other end of the wealth and income scale, the 20 to 25 percent of the population living at or below the "poverty line" persist in that state pri-

TABLE IV Percentage Distribution of Stock Ownership and Value of Stockholdings Within Income Groups (1962)

		Value of Stockholdings			
Family Income	None	*Less than $500*	*$500–$999*	*$1,000–$4,999*	*$5,000 and over*
Below $3,000	95%	1%	1%	1%	2%
$3,000–$4,999	91	2	1	2	4
$5,000–$7,499	87	3	2	4	4
$7,500–$9,999	78	5	2	8	7
$10,000–$14,999	62	4	6	13	15
$15,000 and over	33	4	1	8	44
All families	84	3	1	5	7

SOURCE: Survey Research Center, *1964 Survey of Consumer Finances* (Ann Arbor, Mich.: Braun-Brumfield, 1965), Table 6-1, p. 96.

marily because of these same institutionalized arrangements for the ownership and control of property—the resources and productive forces of the society.[4] It has been known for some time that the amount of resources and productive facilities of American society is quite sufficient for a fully adequate income for all; it is rather the conventional arrangements of control and distribution that account primarily for the shape of the distribution of income and wealth that our charts and figures show. It would be a mistake, therefore, to view the concentration of wealth simply in terms of its possible redistribution to the lower segments of society, since this would only amount to a few dollars addition to their incomes. Rather, the greater significance of the concentration of wealth lies in the very great stakes in and the heavy psychological commitment to the existing institutionalized property arrangements on the part of the upper-income and wealth-holding groups. The result is the strong conservative force in most of the controlling centers of the country, especially economic and political, which underlies the "cold war" foreign policy and has so far successfully prevented any of those more significant changes in the institutionalized economic control arrangements at home that would be necessary to eradicate the socially structured poverty affecting about one-fifth of the members of the society. The typical official response to socially structured poverty has taken the form of "welfare" programs calling for a redistribution of a very small percentage of the national wealth. But this discussion leads directly to the topic of power and its distribution, which we shall take up in Chapter VI.

We turn now to another measure of economic inequality, the relative shares of the total national income received by the various income-level segments of the population. In the early 1950s a number of writings attempted to propagate what has turned out to be a myth, namely, that since the Depression of the 1930s the United States had seen a large-scale "income revolution" which leveled off incomes to a significant degree and thus greatly reduced inequality.[5] What had in fact happened was that, due to the economic boom created largely by World War II, the real incomes of most groups had increased. Until the 1950s the incomes of lower-class working groups had increased at a faster rate than those of higher-income groups, but since then a reversal of the trend has almost wiped out the relative change. To put it simply, the size of the economic pie increased, but as Table V indicates, the way the pie is divided up has not shown any radical change. Thus since 1937 the share of the lowest income tenth has fluctuated very little around 1 percent of the national personal income, while the share of the highest tenth seems to have decreased slightly from about 34 percent to between 27 and 30 percent. And even this small shift has been attributed not to a real shift in income but to a change in income-reporting habits made possible by "loopholes" in the income tax laws favoring the underreporting of real income by the higher income levels. But assuming that Table V reflects accurate income figures, it suggests that the drop in percentage of the highest tenth is reflected in a gain for the next two or three higher tenths but has not led to any redistribution for the lower half of income earners.

As has been pointed out, the main social significance of

TABLE V Percent of National Personal Income Before Taxes Received by Each Income Tenth

Year	Highest Tenth	2nd Tenth	3rd Tenth	4th Tenth	5th Tenth	6th Tenth	7th Tenth	8th Tenth	9th Tenth	Lowest Tenth
1910	34%	12%	10%	9%	8%	7%	6%	6%	5%	3%
1918	35	13	10	9	8	7	7	6	4	2
1921	38	13	10	9	7	7	6	5	3	2
1929	39	12	10	9	8	7	6	5	4	2
1937	34	14	12	10	9	7	6	4	3	1
1948	31	15	12	10	9	8	6	5	3	1
1950	29	15	13	11	9	8	6	5	3	1
1952	30	15	12	11	9	8	6	5	3	1
1954	29	15	12	11	9	8	6	5	3	1
1956	31	15	12	11	9	8	6	5	3	1
1958	27	16	13	11	9	8	6	5	3	1
1960	28	16	13	11	9	8	6	5	3	1
1962	27	16	13	11	9	8	7	5	3	1
1964	30	15	13	11	9	8	6	4	3	1

SOURCE: Data for 1910–1937 are from the National Industrial Conference Board, *Studies in Enterprise and Social Progress* (New York: National Industrial Conference Board, 1939), p. 125, given here in rounded form. Data for 1948–1964 are reproduced from *Survey of Consumer Finances,* 1954, 1961, 1963, and 1967, by permission of Survey Research Center, University of Michigan, Ann Arbor.

differential distribution of income, wealth, and occupation lies in the fact that it results in inequalities of opportunity: it affects the chances of people at various levels to obtain desired values. The effects of economic differences on specific life chances and life situations must therefore be examined.

CLASS DIFFERENCES IN LIFE EXPECTANCY, HEALTH, AND MENTAL DISORDER

Even the most basic chance, the chance to stay alive, is related to one's social class. The statistical evidence shows that the traditional class gap in mortality has narrowed in all Western countries in recent years but significant differentials in life expectancy remain. In the United States the average infant born today can look forward to a life span of about seventy years. A study undertaken in Baltimore in 1949–1951, however, showed the following life expectancies at birth.[6]

	Class*					
	I Highest	*II*	*III*	*IV*	*V Lowest*	*Difference Between I and V*
White males	68.5 years	66.4	65.4	63.9	61.4	7.1
White females	73.1	72.4	71.2	69.8	68.4	4.7

* Class refers to the division of the city census tracts into quintiles based on the median rental in each tract.

Although the difference is smaller among females than among males, the inverse relationship is clear for both sexes and the differences between the highest and the lowest class are considerable.

Major differences have also been shown by the most sophisticated and elaborate investigation of mortality differentials undertaken to date. This research was based upon a large nationwide sample of deaths occurring in the United States in 1960. A preliminary analysis of the data for white persons has been reported but not yet published.[7] It shows that both income and education are inversely related. Among white males twenty-five to sixty-four years old, mortality for those with family incomes below $2,000 was 2.5 times higher than for those with family incomes of more than $10,000. For females the corresponding differential was 2 to 1. Educational differentials were likewise great: the mortality level among men twenty-five to sixty-four years old with no schooling was 56 percent higher than that for men with one or more years of college. And for white women twenty-five to sixty-four years old with no schooling it was twice as high as for women with some college training.

There is also evidence that the wealthier live healthier lives than the poor. Thus a National Health Survey made in the early 1960s found substantially higher rates of certain chronic physical disabilities among the lowest-income groups, including heart conditions, hypertension, arthritis and rheumatism, and visual and hearing impairments.[8] Hospitalization, measured in terms of rate of hospital discharges, was lowest for members of families with incomes of $10,000 and over (116.5 per 1,000 population) and highest for the lowest-income groups (136.4 per 1,000 for the under-$2,000 group and 145.6 per 1,000 for the $2,000–$4,000 group).[9] The rates of restricted activity, bed disability, and time lost from work showed a similar pattern, with the under-$2,000-family-income group having approximately twice the rates on all of these compared with the $10,000 and over group.[10]

The evidence shows class differentials not only in physical disabilities but also in mental health. The survey cited above, for example, found that 9.2 percent of the persons sampled with family incomes of less than $2,000 reported mental and nervous conditions, whereas the $7,000 and over group reported 5.4 percent of such conditions. A large-scale study of the relation between stratification and psychiatric disorders reported that the wealthiest class of New Haven, Connecticut, made up 3 percent of that city's total population but contributed only 1 percent of the disorders being treated by a psychiatrist in 1950.[11] Semiskilled factory hands and unskilled laborers, on the other hand, who constituted 18 percent of the community's population, contributed 37 percent of the psychiatric patients. The study also indicated that the type of psychiatric treatment a mental patient received was closely associated with his class position. The percentage of patients who received only custodial care without active treatment was greater in the lower classes, while psychotherapy, for example, was concentrated in the higher classes. Thus both the individual's likelihood of becoming mentally ill and his chances of receiving active treatment and recovering quickly seemed to be closely related to his position in the class structure.

However, mental health has become an area of research subject to much debate concerning the validity and interpretation of findings and will require further study before firm conclusions can be reached.

CLASS AND EDUCATION

Except for the possibility of staying alive and remaining healthy the most crucial life chance in our society is probably the opportunity to obtain a good education, especially a higher education. As American society has become more and more urbanized and industrialized, the educational requirements for the higher-paid and otherwise more desirable occupations have increased. Thus the amount of formal education an individual receives has come to be a major determinant of the occupation he can enter and the amount of income he will be able to command. This widely understood situation is documented by a report based on 1960 census data,[12] which demonstrates the relationship between amount of schooling and occupational achievement and monetary success. For example, the figures bring out that of all men twenty-five years and over about 87 percent of those with less than five years of elementary schooling and 82 percent of those with eight years of elementary schooling are concentrated in manual labor and farm work. High school graduates occupy a transitional position between manual labor and white-collar occupations: 56 percent of the men who completed four years of high school held manual jobs, many of them skilled craftsmen and foremen, but a substantial proportion were sales and clerical workers (18 percent) and in managerial positions (15 percent).

Those who attended but did not finish college, the figures show, are concentrated in clerical and managerial positions, only about one-quarter of them being engaged in professional or technical work (22 percent); one-third hold blue-collar jobs, approximately half of those being highly skilled craftsmen. The greatest contrast in occupational achievement is between those who drop out of college and college graduates—57 percent of the latter are in professional and technical occupations and another 18 percent are business managers or proprietors. The 1960 census report also contains some enlightening data on the relationship between formal education and money income (see Table VI).

TABLE VI Relationship Between Formal Education and Money Income (1959)

All Males		*Median Income of Males 25 Years and over*
No school years completed		$1,439
Elementary:	1 to 4 years	$1,844
	5 to 7 years	$3,062
	8 years	$3,885
High School:	1 to 3 years	$4,847
	4 years	$5,437
College:	1 to 3 years	$5,980
	4 years	$7,646
Total		$4,617

SOURCE: *1960 Census of Population,* Vol. I: *Characteristics of the Population, Part A, U.S. Summary,* Table 223, p. 1–590.

The positive correlation between number of years of school completed and average income is quite clear. Especially striking is the financial advantage of those who have a completed college education. The latter received almost 50 percent more income than high school graduates and twice the income of those with only eight years of elementary school.

Perhaps more revealing is a Census Bureau estimate of the total money value of schooling made by calculating the approximate lifetime incomes of men at different educational levels (see Table VII).

According to this estimate a college degree appears to be worth $135,000 more than a high school diploma, which in turn is worth $50,000 more than a completed elementary school education. These are only rough estimates, of course, subject to changing conditions, but they illustrate the improved earning power associated with each additional increment of education.

TABLE VII Lifetime Income of Males 25–64 Years (1961)

Years of School Completed	*Lifetime Income*
0–7	$124,930
8	168,810
9–11	193,082
12	224,417
13–15	273,049
16 years and over	360,604

SOURCE: U.S. Bureau of the Census, *Statistical Abstract of the United States: 1963* (Washington, D.C.: Government Printing Office, 1963), p. 122.

Since it is clear, then, that formal schooling is a major factor in determining the type of occupation open to an individual and the amount of remuneration he can expect to receive for his work, it would seem of utmost importance in a democratic society that the educational system select and encourage those with the best abilities, regardless of their social origin. There can be no equality of opportunity if there is unequal access to education, especially higher education. This principle is well recognized in our equalitarian ideology and the traditional tenet that "education must give all boys and girls their chance."

However, educational opportunities are not in fact equally available to all. The chances of a young person's going to college are especially affected by his parents' occupational and economic status. Thus in the early 1960s about two-thirds of the American young people reaching eighteen graduated from high school and about half of these entered college, with 60 percent of the entrants finishing and receiving degrees. Parents with family incomes of less than $5,000, making up about 47 percent of all families, contributed about a quarter of the college students between the ages of twenty and twenty-four in 1960. Parents with incomes between $5,000 and $7,500—about 25 percent of the total—contributed their share of another quarter of the students. Families with incomes between $7,500 and $10,000—around 13 percent of all families—accounted for about 21 percent of the college students, and the 15 percent of families with incomes over $10,000 contributed 29 percent.[13]

Viewed more generally, the 1960 census data show that 9 percent of all families with less than $5,000 income had children in college, the figure progressively rising to 44 percent for families with $10,000 income and over. But the data also show that the level of education of the parents, apart from their income, is an important factor in determining college attendance for the children. Thus, of fathers who did not finish high school only 11 percent had children in college, whereas of the fathers who themselves attended college, 51 percent contributed children to the college population.[14] If a man has gone to college, then, he is much more likely to send his children to college regardless of income.

It can be surmised from the above figures that a good deal of talent is not being tapped. Although brighter youngsters tend to go to college regardless of income of parents, a good proportion—some say about a third—do not receive any higher education.[15]

In recent years noteworthy efforts have been made to provide higher education at low cost to able students. State universities have expanded their facilities, private colleges are providing substantial funds for scholarships, and the federal government has made educational grants to large numbers of veterans. The effects of these measures have undoubtedly increased the chances of children with superior intelligence from lower economic groups to obtain a college education, but great inequalities still remain. Thus a study of the socioeconomic background of students enrolled at the University of Indiana in 1946–1947 brings out once more the familiar relationship between fathers' occupation and sons' college attendance: professional fathers contributed 14 percent of the students while making up only 4 percent of the state's population, while sons of semiskilled and unskilled workers, constituting 44 percent of the population, represented but 13 percent of the student body. A comparison of veterans with students without military service also showed that the GI Bill of Rights increased the proportion of students from the lower occupational groups attending the university by more than 90 percent.[16]

Substantially similar results were obtained in a survey of the types of schools attended by the sixteen- and seventeen-year-old children of the residents of New Haven, Connecticut, in 1949.[17] Dividing the city's population into six social classes, this research indicates that 43 percent of the children of the lowest class had already dropped out of school while over 98 percent of the highest-class children were still attending school. Moreover, the three higher classes were overrepresented in all types of postsecondary schools and in private schools but underrepresented in vocational trade school, while the reverse held of the lower classes. The study came to the conclusion "that in a contemporary New England city the social class membership of one's family determines, in part, not only the length of time one will attend school but also the particular type of school attended. . . . [The child's] pattern of schooling is partially determined by the mere fact of his birth into a family of a particular social class status." [18]

To a large extent the prevailing inequalities of educational opportunity, documented by these and many other studies, are the direct result of economic factors which force many children from lower-income groups to drop out of high school in order to earn a living and prevent the majority of them from going to college even if they manage to complete high school. But differences in financial circumstances are not the whole explanation, for children from lower socioeconomic groups often leave school because they are discriminated against and discouraged by superintendents, principals, teachers, and more fortunate classmates.

Investigations of the school systems of various American communities have revealed the existence of a number of discriminatory practices. One study of a midwestern small town ("Elmtown") high school, for example, shows that good grades are biased in favor of students from "better" homes while failures of lower-class students are much more frequent than the IQ differentials between the classes would lead one to expect—and intelligence tests themselves are known to favor children from upper-class homes. Elmtown's superintendents, principals, and teachers were reported to discriminate not only in grading but in the award of prizes and honors, the administration of school discipline, and in extracurricular activities sponsored by the school, often under direct and open pressure from higher-class parents.[19] Small wonder that the "better"-class students themselves also discriminated against children from poorer homes in their social activities. Similarly, a study of a New England city revealed the deliberate efforts of a grammar school principal to dissuade lower-class students from selecting college preparatory high school courses and to "change the minds" of those who did not see the light.[20]

It would be unfair, however, to attribute the early withdrawal of lower-class children from school entirely to frustrating circumstances. The cultural milieu of lower-class homes also often obstructs the educational development of their children. Many working-class parents do not extol the virtues of education, emphasizing rather the importance of going to work and contributing to the family's income. Under such circumstances children with the requisite ability for higher education may lack the necessary aspiration and motivation to go on to college. A study of high school students in the Boston area shows that the occupational choices of highly intelligent boys from working-class homes are strongly influenced by parental pressures. Working-class parents who are discontented with their way of life, this study stresses, train their children to regard education seriously and to want to go on to college as a means of "bettering themselves." On the other hand, parents who are satisfied with their jobs and way of life emphasize a philosophy of "getting by" rather than "getting ahead" and are apt to encourage in their sons attitudes critical of or unsympathetic to the idea of a college education.[21]

Such findings sometimes lead to the conclusion that large numbers of able children from working-class backgrounds would not take advantage of opportunities to obtain a higher education even if sufficient financial resources were made available to them. While there is some truth in this view, its exponents frequently overlook the fact that working-class attitudes unfavorable to education are often the result of parents' ignorance and limited perspective: because the parents lack knowledge of educational opportunities, they advise their children to "study something practical" and to get a job as soon as possible. Here is a vicious circle: lack of educational experience on the part of the parents results in ignorance of opportunities, and parental ignorance in turn encourages the children to pass up chances of a higher education.

THE ADMINISTRATION OF JUSTICE AND LEGAL PROTECTION

We pointed out earlier that one of the main characteristics of modern class systems is the absence, officially, of legal privileges and legal distinctions between different classes. "Equality of all citizens before the law" is one of the basic principles of our social order, but as with equality of opportunity, practices differ considerably from the ideal.

Although the data are scanty and unsystematic, there is strong evidence of class bias in the administration of justice and legal protection in our society. Individuals of the higher economic and occupational levels escape arrest and conviction to a greater extent than lower-class persons, even when equally guilty of crimes. Although this may seem a shocking state of affairs it is not surprising, since it costs money to ask for justice. Wealthy persons can employ the best legal talent and, at times, expert witnesses. They can exercise personal influence to escape arrest or conviction, obtain changes of venue and delays, and if found guilty they are often fined rather than imprisoned. Poor people, on the other hand, are more likely to be arrested and remanded to jail if they cannot furnish bail. Without financial and political power they cannot defend themselves as effectively when on trial and are more likely to be convicted.

Statistics of arrests in a New England city ("Yankee City") provide clear evidence of class differences in liability to or protection from arrest by the local police. Almost 90 percent of arrests in Yankee City were of members of the two lowest classes, which constituted 58 percent of the population of this presumably six-class community. The members of the two highest classes, totaling only 3 percent of the population, contributed less than three-fourths of 1 percent of the arrests.[22] Although members of the lower classes violate certain laws more frequently, interviews with the law enforcement officers indicated "that the same acts committed in the higher and lower classes resulted in fewer arrests for those who were better placed socially." [23]

A similar situation is reported in a study of a small South Dakota town. Here it was found that "local police officials are expected to deal severely with Bottoms delinquents on the theory that they come from bad stock and must be deterred, therefore, through strict punishment. Offenders from the Tops are deemed 'accidental' or 'queer' cases that in no way reflect on their families and consequently are released after warning." [24] Clearly, then, the implementation of the law differs according to the class position of the offender.

In addition to this class-biased administration of the law in the case of offenses committed by persons, there is also evidence of bias in the administration of criminal justice under laws that pertain exclusively to business and the professions and that therefore apply primarily to middle- and upper-class individuals. Many business practices involve legally punishable offenses which are not detected or are not severely dealt with by the courts. These violations of law, conveniently called white-collar crimes because they are committed by persons of social respectability in the course of their occupational activities, include such criminal offenses as violations of the anti-trust laws and of maximum-price regulations, unfair labor practices, financial manipulations, and fraudulent advertising.[25] Offenses of this kind are frequent and their financial cost is higher than that of "ordinary" crimes, but the offenders (often corporations) are usually not considered "criminals" by the public, and convictions generally result in fines which mean relatively little to businessmen of means or to large corporations.

THE HIERARCHY OF CLASSES

The foregoing discussion underscores the presence of marked differentials in income, wealth, and occupation in American society and traces their effects on certain life chances of individuals. Economic inequalities strongly influence, as we have shown, the opportunities of individuals to stay healthy and survive, their prospects of getting a higher education, and their chances of obtaining justice and legal protection.

Moreover, study of the statistical data presented in the foregoing sections indicates that these are not merely matters of individual inequalities and differentials but that whole segments of the population are in similar economic positions and therefore have similar chances and opportunities. This statistical evidence of the differential distribution of life chances and economic positions may be used to trace the main lines of the class hierarchy and to mark the broad boundaries of the various classes in this country.

Combining the statistical information from Tables I, II, and III with the other data presented above, we can distinguish a hierarchical arrangement of three major classes in American society, which for some purposes can be further subdivided. Numerically largest is the bottom segment, the *working class,* since it consists of skilled, semiskilled and unskilled urban manual workers, farm laborers, and some categories of farm tenants. As Table II shows, it comprises about 58 percent of the population.

At the other end of the scale is a numerically small but influential *upper class* of big businessmen and top corporation officials. It is difficult to estimate their numbers but it is probably not too wide of the mark to equate them with the select 0.8 percent of the population whose annual incomes exceed $25,000 (see Table I).

Between these two extremes is the *middle class,* a large and heterogeneous aggregate of small businessmen, independent farmers, professionals, intellectuals, and a host of salaried white-collar employees.

It should be clearly understood that this is a broad and rough classification. Because of the dynamic fluidity of our stratification system and the high degree of social mobility, which we shall examine in some detail in Chapter VIII, the boundaries between these three major classes are not sharp and clear-cut. Furthermore, for many purposes this classification is too broad, and therefore subdivisions of the three major classes must be used in the analysis of certain problems.

Within the upper class, for example, we can distinguish an elite that exercises decisive political and economic power. This active upper-class elite, as we shall see in Chapter VI, consists largely of major corporation executives and is recruited mainly from the upper class, but it is a fairly open and shifting elite which is reinforced by and sprinkled with members of the professions, the military, and professional politics. In general, there is no clear break between the upper class as a whole and the upper reaches of the middle class; they shade into each other. In some respects, therefore, the dividing line between the upper and middle classes is less significant than the subdivision within the latter between the so-called upper-middle class and lower-middle class.

The criteria for distinguishing the upper-middle and lower-middle class are complex. In addition to occupation they include status within the occupation, measured largely by the degree of personal independence and security in work and by opportunity for the exercise of authority as well as the amount and source of income. These indexes suggest that the upper-middle class consists essentially of the owners and executives of medium-sized businesses, their better-paid salaried employees, and many professionals. The lower-middle class includes small businessmen, clerks and clerical workers, many (not all) salesmen, minor employed professionals and semiprofessionals, and the bulk of the civil servants. One good index of the line between the upper-middle and the lower-middle class is the expectation of upper-middle-class children that all of them, regardless of sex, will receive a college education as a matter of birthright. The more limited funds of lower-middle-class parents, on the other hand, mean that only those children with superior ability can count on a college education with reasonable certainty. Where they have several children to educate, lower-middle-class families frequently find it necessary to favor the boys, who receive a four-year college program, while the girls must content themselves with a shorter and less expensive education. Keeping in mind such factors, as well as the fact that any dividing line is necessarily arbitrary, it is reasonable to assume that families with incomes between $10,000 and $25,000 (14.2 percent; see Table I) constitute the upper-middle class.

As we shall see in the discussion of social mobility, there is ample evidence that the major class division in the United States, as in other Western societies, is that between the middle class as a whole and the lower or working class. This is largely a division between manual labor and white-collar occupations.

However, this contrast is less visible here than in other countries because a large part of the working class shares a "white-collar" style of life and accepts middle-class values and beliefs (see Chapter V). The latter situation holds especially for many craftsmen, foremen, and skilled mechanics, whose high wages nowadays exceed the salaries of many lower-middle-class white-collar employees and even of small businessmen (see Table III). In many respects, therefore, the line that sets off the "aristocracy of skilled labor" from the bulk of semiskilled and unskilled manual laborers is more significant sociologically than the dividing line between skilled craftsmen and lower-middle-class white-collar workers, which has become increasingly blurred in recent years.

A special word should be added about the place of independent farmers in our class structure. As Tables I and III show, the money income of these agrarian enterprisers ranks at the very bottom of the scale, with the sole exception of the farm laborers whom they employ. It should be realized, however, that these data cannot be taken at their face value, since an important proportion of farm income is often obtained in kind rather than money, indicating that the income of farmers is probably understated. With respect to both their income and wealth, as well as their style of life, the vast majority of American farmers may be considered as small business enterprisers and members of the lower-middle class.

To repeat, the class hierarchy outlined above is based upon a definition of classes as aggregates of individuals and families who are in similar economic positions and therefore have similar opportunities and life chances. This classification does not permit any inference concerning awareness or consciousness of class position or the beliefs and values which members of classes may hold. Nor does it take into consideration the power relations that exist between classes. As we have pointed out, these dimensions of stratification, to be sure, are closely related to class position; but they must be analyzed separately. Therefore we next examine the way in which the economic position of

Americans is connected with their chances of participating in the nonmaterial culture, their prospects of attaining prestige and influence, and their opportunities to exercise authority and power.

V

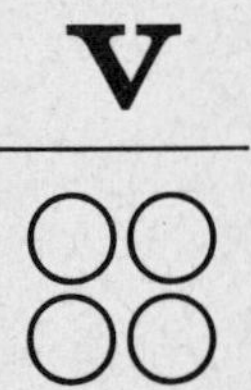

Prestige, Style of Life, and Status Groups in American Society

The differential distribution of income, wealth, and life chances, which divides our society into several classes, is also reflected in differences of social prestige of the individuals and families who compose these classes. However, as was pointed out in Chapter IV, the status hierarchy is not identical with the class order. Prestige ranking involves interpersonal evaluation, the criteria for evaluation including both such objective class factors as income, wealth, power, occupation, and education and the cultural attributes and characteristic forms of behavior in which these objective conditions find expression. Claims for prestige are therefore based not only on the amount of money an individual possesses but also on the way he uses it, his style of life, and the length of time his family has been able to live in a given style, or colloquially, on his "background" and "breeding."

In time objective circumstances create distinctive cultural likenesses among persons similarly situated and become the basis of social group formations. Several thorough studies of American communities, made in the 1930s and 1940s, including "Middletown," "Yankee City," "Plainville," and "Elmtown," indicate that differences in occupation, income, wealth, and education lead to the formation of local status groups which display consistently different forms of behavior and which have different ideas, attitudes, values, and tastes, and that these differences form the basis for invidious rank evaluations.[1]

In these various communities the investigators found that individuals and families confine their social relationships, particularly the more intimate ones, largely to others with similar cultural characteristics and that these groups are differently evaluated by local people in terms of prestige—that is, they tend to form a status hierarchy. Such local status hierarchies have their own peculiarities and vary in size and complexity from one community to another. While we cannot consider the details of these several community investigations, at least a few of the findings, which highlight significant differences in the cultural attributes and the styles of life that characterize different status groups and form the basis of local prestige hierarchies, should be summarized.

FORMAL AND INFORMAL ASSOCIATIONS AND PARTICIPATION

We may begin by examining the extent to which formal association and informal group participation function to divide the residents of American communities into disparate and exclusive status groups. Considering, first, participation in formally organized voluntary associations, the cliché depicting Americans as "a nation of joiners" needs considerable modification. To be sure, this country abounds with innumerable secret societies, fraternities, lodges, and civic organizations which serve a great variety of purposes, but the majority of the population has few or no affiliations with formally organized associations.

Membership in such organizations differs strikingly according to occupation and income. A study of organized group affiliations in New York City reported that only thirty-two of every one hundred unskilled workers in the sample belonged to any organizations, whereas 67 percent of the businessmen and 98 percent of the professionals earning more than $5,000 (in the 1940s) annually listed one or more organizational affiliations.[2] A similar pattern was discovered in "Yankee City," where approximately 72 percent of the members of the upper class belonged to associations as compared with 53 percent of the middle class and 32 percent of the lower class.[3] An investigation of the associational memberships of a group of semi-skilled workers and their families in New Haven, Connecticut, reveals that 90 percent had no ties with formally organized associations.[4]

"Joining," then, is more prevalent among members of the middle and the upper classes than elsewhere in the class structure. This does not mean, of course, that working-class people live in social isolation. As the New Haven study illustrates, however, the active social life of most working-class persons is largely confined to informal leisure-time activities that take place in intimate cliques made up primarily of relatives.[5]

The sharp class differences in the proportion of those who are joiners are no more important, sociologically, than the differences in the types of association to which members of different classes belong. While it is true that membership in some national organizations, for example, the American Legion, cuts across classes in a community, each class is marked by a typical pattern of associations. Upper-class men join such groups as historical societies and exclusive social clubs, while their wives are members of a variety of "cultural," educational, and charitable organizations. Upper-middle-class men belong to Masonic and service organizations, like Rotary, Kiwanis, and Lions, and to occupational and professional associations. White-collar clerical employees and working-class people, on the other hand, belong mainly to fraternal lodges, patriotic groups, labor unions, and religious organizations, while their wives form the "auxiliaries" of these associations.

To some extent, this differentiation of associations according to class includes religious organization. In the United States the separation of church and state helps to make participation in religious activities a voluntary matter and the churches, therefore, are similar in organizational makeup to other voluntary associations. This is especially evident in the case of the many Protestant denominations which are no longer as separated by doctrinal differences as by the class and status differences of their members. In some measure their members are recruited along class and status lines. Individual Protestant churches are often "class churches," and each denomination, while it usually includes members from several social levels, is to a certain extent associated with one particular class.[6] Thus Episcopalians, Presbyterians, and Congregationalists (and Unitarians in New England) have tended, at least in the past, to be upper and upper-middle class, Methodists and Lutherans middle class, and Baptists and members of evangelical and revivalist sects lower class. Generally, church affiliation itself has been most characteristic of middle-class people, who not only join but go to church, giving some ground to the claim that active church membership is essentially a middle-class phenomenon.

If formal associations—with their officers, bylaws, and rules of admittance—serve to divide the group life of a community along class lines, this division is even more pronounced in the informal groups and cliques that have no explicitly stated regulations or officers but are notoriously effective in controlling the behavior of their members. The informal and intimate association of people who eat together, visit and gossip, and intermarry leads, in fact, to the formation of fundamental status groups in American communities. Through informal associations and cliques the diffuse likenesses of individuals of similar occupation, with similar shares of the scarce values of our society, are translated into effective group solidarity and social interaction. Participation in these "social sets," "crowds," or "gangs" largely depends upon the possession of the "right" status symbols and the "correct" background and behavior. These informal groups determine and circumscribe the type and character of the individual's intimate social relationships, they control much of his conduct, and, as various studies show, their membership is usually—though not always—limited to people of the same economic positions.[7]

In a 1963 study of a sample of residents of two cities making up part of a metropolitan area in the Eastern United States, Edward O. Laumann investigated the degree to which intimate interaction is structured by occupational rank.[8] Occupational status was assumed to be both objectively basic in determining a person's position in the stratification system and subjectively important as an informational cue by which people perceive others and decide whether or not they will make attractive interactional partners. Laumann found that comparable occupational status was the main factor in determining the persons with whom one actually engages in a variety of more intimate social relationships, although preferences of all class levels tended toward those of higher occupational prestige than themselves. An important finding was that friendship interaction was most strongly based on equal-status considerations, compared with intermarriage or relations based on social origin or neighborhood. This suggests that friendship patterns might be an especially important focus in the maintenance of the class and status structure, since such patterns are found to be strongly related to one's attitudes, beliefs, and behaviors concerning class, status, economics, and politics.

Laumann's study is also important in confirming that there are identifiable clusterings of intimate interaction among occupational groupings. At the top and the bottom of the occupational prestige hierarchy the groupings are found to be especially crystallized in the form of circumscribed intimate relationships and in terms of the perceptions of persons of all levels that at these occupational extremes there are powerful "ingroups." On the other hand, the middle occupational categories showed a considerable amount of fluidity in intimate interactions and subjective preferences. However, class-based groupings could be found, though they did not have the clear-cut and publicly agreed-upon identities of the more extreme groups. The fluidity and heterogeneity of intimate interactions in the middle levels are important factors that help to explain the lack of an exact correlation between occupational status and economic and political beliefs and attitudes. Thus, as the theoretical framework presented in Chapter III suggested, close interaction across class or occupational status levels tends to prevent the crystallization or perpetuation of well-defined class subcultures. Nevertheless, as this framework also makes clear, intimate social interaction is not the only important factor defining or structuring social classes; the latter are also shaped by differential positions in the economic structure of society, which in turn determine life chances—the differential constraints and opportunities that tend to segregate groupings in society.

VALUE ORIENTATIONS AND CONSUMPTION PATTERNS

Participation in formal and informal associations, although a useful index, is not the only evidence of status differences. The whole range of people's behavior and outlook, their entire way of life, varies among the upper, lower, and middle levels of the status hierarchy. Some of these differences are apparent, while others are more subtle, requiring close scrutiny. A large body of research permits us to generalize about these differences, but the reader should keep in mind the fact that our generalizations admit many exceptions.

Outstanding among the highly visible status symbols is residence. Most American towns have a right and a wrong "side of the tracks"—their "best," "good," and "poor" residential sections. This geographical division, to be sure, is largely the product of the financial position and occupational activity of the various segments of the population, but the area of residence and the type of dwelling also reflect the tendency of higher status groups to translate social distance into physical distance. A spacious house set in a well-kept garden with wide lawns on a broad residential street is an expression of "gracious living" which symbolizes upper-class or upper-middle-class status. The lower-middle class, and increasingly large numbers of skilled workingmen, live in one- or two-family houses, with small yards or gardens, located on side streets or in the rapidly mushrooming suburban developments. Many working-class families, however, still cannot afford better housing than the crowded apartments and tenements that line so many drab and dingy city streets or, increasingly, sardine-packed "suburbs" at the fringes of large cities. Moving into a better residential section is an important way of expressing status aspirations, not only because the move represents an outward sign of success but also because residential location helps to determine informal associations. (We do not imply that people change residence *merely* to improve their social status. The determinants of social behavior are many and complex and, in this case, include the search for cleanliness, space, better schools, and so on.)

Residence is merely one symbol of the cultural differences which are reflected in the standard of living and pattern of consumption of different status levels. The possession of money obviously is a requirement for high status, but knowing how to spend it can be at least as important. Money must be transformed into specific patterns of behavior and possessions if specific status claims are to be made.

An upper-class style of life thus includes not only a fine home staffed with "domestics" but also large expenditures for travel and philanthropy. Upper-class children are sent to private "finishing" and "prep" schools and (if they can meet the increasingly rigorous entrance requirements) the "name" colleges and universities. Leisure-time and recreational activities have traditionally included polo, yachting, and other sports that cannot be easily imitated by those on lower rungs of the status ladder, although this pattern has been changing somewhat with the growing "democratization" of sports.

It should be noted, however, that older, well-established, and more secure segments of the upper class do not indulge in the ostentatious display and conspicuous consumption typical of the late-nineteenth-century "gilded age," satirized by Thorstein Veblen and more recently depicted by Cleveland Amory.[9] Flashy cars and fashionable clothes are the badge of "café society" and the *nouveaux riches*. This is understandable in a country that lacks an old-established aristocracy and titled nobility, where conspicuous display of wealth enables the newly "arrived" to document his success. But the "old families" do not need to advertise their established and widely recognized wealth and social standing. Thus they emphasize conservative attitudes concerning social issues, restrained and cultivated tastes, and quiet unobtrusive manners.

The upper-middle-class style of life accents material well-being. Members of this group live in comfortable homes, drive good cars, and provide superior education for their children. They can afford to cultivate intellectual and artistic interests. But they place less emphasis on elaborate social rituals and are less preoccupied with the historical and genealogical matters that are often the hobbies of many upper-class families. Upper-middle-class people are more concerned with the future than with the past, they strive for success in business or the professions, and many are civic leaders. Some of them probably aspire to social acceptance by the upper class and feel disappointed if they do not succeed,[10] but many others seem to be well content with their status.

If security and comfort are characteristic of the upper reaches of the middle class, insecurity and anxiety are frequent features of lower-middle-class life. The predominant white-collar occupations of the members of this group encourage psychological identification with the upper and upper-middle class, who are often their employers; but their incomes are generally not much higher, if at all, than those of manual workers. Thus they are anxious to set themselves off from the working class through their manner of living: their small houses are apt to be immaculate and furnished according to the prescription of, say, *Better Homes and Gardens*. Their lawns are trim and neat and their cars carefully polished, if not new. They emphasize respectability and a relatively rigid morality, tending to be even more conservative than the upper class in these respects.

The lower-middle class probably contains the largest proportion of people striving to "move up" economically and socially. Many are discontent with their status and therefore highly value self-improvement, attending lectures and reading books and magazines in the hope of making a better place for themselves or at least for their children. Their anxiety to get ahead sometimes provokes the label of "strainers" or strivers. But it has also been claimed, with some justification perhaps, that the behavior patterns and value system of the lower-middle class represent the core culture of the "American way of life." [11]

Certainly the American tradition of striving for success and upward mobility, so strongly embodied in the lower-middle-class way of life, extends its sway over many manual workers who share traditional middle-class values. The style of life of many skilled and better-paid semiskilled workers resembles that of the lower-middle class much more closely than that of the poorer semiskilled and unskilled manual laborers. The higher wages of recent years have enabled many workingmen to buy their own houses and to furnish them much like those of white-collar people, whom they also resemble by stressing respectability, sobriety, church membership, and mobility aspirations. Away from the job, they cannot be distinguished from the lower-middle-class white-collar men.

However, not all manual workers have been able or willing to adopt a middle-class style of life. The still sizable though continuously decreasing segment of unskilled laborers and migratory farm workers leads lives characterized by poverty, dilapidated housing, shabby clothing, and recurring bouts of unemployment. These people are too poor to entertain much hope for a better future. But many better-paid semiskilled workers as well are not strongly motivated by the desire to get ahead and care little for the symbols and values of middle-class culture. Their behavior patterns and moral standards differ markedly from the middle-class pattern. Having limited education, they show little interest in "cultural" activities, are infrequent "joiners," and are relatively unconcerned with "respectability"—they live for the present, which they do not care to mortgage for an uncertain future.

Recent criticisms of this thesis of *embourgeoisement*—the view that the working class in industrial society, largely due to the affluence of recent decades, has lost its identity as a separate class and has largely merged into the middle class in terms of its attitudes and style of life—bring out further important considerations.[12] For one thing, there has been a growing discrepancy between the conditions of the working class while "on the job" and during leisure time. Increasing job security and rising levels of living have allowed especially the younger workers to engage in a range of leisure pursuits and consumption patterns that substantially overlap those of the middle class. On the other hand, at work there is still a large element of authoritarian constraint, lack of responsibility, and absence of opportunity for initiative and self-expression. The notion of the worker becoming more middle class is based largely on leisure-time and consumption patterns but fails to consider the different work situation—the relative unity and identification of the middle class with the work authority structure in contrast with the working class. Studies suggest that workers are very much aware of this division in their lives, and as long as it persists their economic and political attitudes will contrast sharply with those of the traditional middle class. Especially at the lower levels of the working class, it is held, a significant degree of alienation from the economic and political authority structure will continue.

In addition, criticism of the *embourgeoisement* thesis has

led to a more dynamic view of both the working and the middle class. Thus it is suggested that there has been a convergence between a "new middle class," which has given up the radical individualism of the old, and a "new working class," which no longer adheres to the former intense union collectivism. Both groups adhere to a moderate "instrumental collectivism" (many middle-class occupations are unionizing at the same time that many working-class groups are shedding their loyalty to unions). Moreover, the working class has become more "family centered" in its concern with family standards of living, children's education, and chances for occupational advancement.

FAMILY PATTERNS AND SEXUAL BEHAVIOR

The reproductive behavior of different social classes has interested students of society for a long time. Plato, for example, complained that the "unworthy" and "undesirable" elements of the population multiply while the "best people" fail to replace their numbers. This plaint has been echoed throughout the ages. In modern times numerous statistical studies have reported the fertility patterns of different classes. With few exceptions the findings have been essentially the same: they have shown an almost universal inverse relationship between social status and fertility—the more fortunate and favorable the social and economic circumstances of a group, the lower its fertility. This reproductive differential reflects differences in group customs, such as age at marriage, and in values and attitudes concerning parenthood and voluntary family limitation.

In recent years, however, indications of some exceptions and changes in the inverse relationship between socioeconomic status and fertility have appeared. Table VIII shows differential fertility statistics for the United States. Panel 1 (see Table VIII) indicates a straight inverse correlation between income and number of children, and Panel 2 portrays fertility

TABLE VIII Fertility Differentials, or Number of Children Born per 1,000 Women 15–44 Years Old (1964)

Panel 1

Money Income of Family	*Number of Children per Thousand*
$10,000 and over	2,402
$7,500–$9,999	2,420
$5,000–$7,499	2,500
$4,000–$4,999	2,527
$3,000–$3,999	2,728
$2,000–$2,999	2,840
Below $1,999	2,877

Panel 2

Years of School Completed by Wife		
College:	4 or more years	2,020
	1 to 3 years	2,180
High School:	4 years	2,245
	1 to 3 years	2,815
Grade School:	8 years	3,161
	less than 8 years	3,583

Panel 3

Husband's Occupation	
Professional, technical, and kindred workers	2,227
Proprietors, managers, and officials	2,553
Clerical and kindred workers	2,085
Sales workers	2,164
Craftsmen, foremen, and kindred workers	2,583
Operatives and kindred workers	2,606
Service workers	2,436
Laborers, except farm and mine	3,170
Farmers and farm managers	3,147
Farm laborers and foremen	3,443

SOURCE: *Current Population Reports,* Series P-20, No. 147 (January 5, 1966), pp. 16 and 17.

differences by educational achievement of the wife. Here, too, the inverse relationship between amount of schooling and fertility is clear. Panel 3, however, which relates fertility to father's occupation, shows larger numbers of children for professional and businessmen, the top categories in the scale, than for clerical and sales workers, who had the lowest fertility rate.

As voluntary family limitation through contraceptive techniques has gradually spread in recent decades from the upper classes through the middle and working classes the traditional inverse relationship between socioeconomic status and fertility has begun to attenuate slightly. Some demographers have even speculated that eventually, with the general adoption of family planning by all classes, a direct relation between status and fertility might appear. Although Panel 3 shows some evidence of a possible development in that direction, it is too early to ascertain whether or not a general reversal of the trend will actually take place in the future.

Class variations are not confined to the number of children brought into this world but extend also to the training which they receive, though child-training habits change so rapidly over the generations that exact class differences at present are not clear. Several studies made in the 1930s and 1940s documented the class differences in child-rearing practices that prevailed at that time.[13] In general (there were many exceptions, of course), lower-class mothers were more permissive in feeding, weaning, and toilet training than middle-class mothers. The latter were more rigid in the development of cleanliness habits, imposed stricter discipline on their children, and expected them to help in the home and to assume responsibilities at an earlier age. Lower-class children stayed up later, played in the streets without supervision, went to the movies more frequently, and were permitted more freedom for their emotional responses. When quite young, middle-class children were taught to be polite and to control physical aggression. But a survey of studies made by Urie Bronfenbrenner strongly suggests that important changes occurred after World War II.[14] There seemed to be a reversal in practices: the middle-class mother became more permissive in infant care and in young child training. Happiness, considerateness, and self-control for the child became stressed, in contrast with a lower-class emphasis on neatness, cleanliness, and obedience. Working-class parents were more apt to rely on physical punishment and methods involving the threat of loss of love. Though the middle-class parents had higher expectations and demands for the child concerning responsibility, self-care, and progress in school, they also reported more acceptance and equalitarianism as compared with the working-class demand for order and obedience.

Recent studies by Melvin Kohn suggest that the different life experiences, and especially the differences in occupational circumstances, give rise to certain important value differences.[15] As part of their occupations, middle-class people are required to exercise greater initiative and wider latitudes of judgment, to manipulate ideas and symbols, and to depend on their own actions for advancement. In contrast, working-class persons are required primarily to follow explicit rules or instructions set down by an authority, to manipulate things rather than ideas, and to depend more on collective, particularly union, action for promotion. These differences show up as parental value orientations and are taught to children. The middle-class parent emphasizes self-direction and greater independence of action in the child, whereas the lower-class parent stresses conformity to external rules and greater constraints on action. These differentials are consistent with Bronfenbrenner's earlier findings, cited above.

Such contrasting practices, it is clear, tend to give rise to different personality traits in children of diverse social origins. These contrasts in the training and upbringing of children, moreover, produce adults who act and think differently, thereby helping to perpetuate class differences in family behavior from one generation to another.

In view of these contrasting child-raising practices, the differences in the length of formal education, and the earlier age at marriage of lower-class women, it is not surprising that distinct patterns of sexual behavior mark different status levels. The wide divergence of behavior patterns in this important area of human life has been given considerable publicity by the researches of the late Alfred C. Kinsey and his colleagues. The sexual habits of males at the lower occupational and educational levels are thus shown to be quite different from those of males at higher-status levels, although the second "Kinsey Report" does not find this contrast in the case of females (probably because of the lower age at marriage and shorter period of schooling of working-class girls. It should also be noted that the very small number of working-class females in the sample raises doubts about the significance of this finding).[16]

Lower-class males, having acquired an intimate and realistic knowledge of the "facts of life" at an early age, often consider sex relations a "natural" part of life. In contrast to the members of the middle class, they place little value on virginity, have premarital intercourse frequently, and do not consider extramarital affairs especially reprehensible. On the other hand, they are apt to look upon petting and other erotic techniques widely practiced at the middle-class and especially the college level as abnormal and perverse. Kinsey's findings have been criticized, primarily because his sample is not representative of the population as a whole, but the overall picture of sexual behavior patterns which emerges from his large-scale researches conforms closely to the reports at that time of other investigators of class differences in sex behavior. Recent studies, however, seem to show important changes in attitudes and values of middle-class youth toward sex, and some little change in actual sex behavior. In addition, many working-class youths appear to be acquiring a broader and more diverse taste in sexual activities.[17]

Various community studies have also brought out the interdependence between marriage and divorce and the class and status system. For example, investigation of the dating behavior of high school students in a small Midwestern city indicates that although dating is a very personal affair it is strongly associated with the daters' positions in the status hierarchy.

The majority of dating relations in this community were reported to take place between persons who belonged to the same prestige level, and when status lines were crossed they usually involved only persons from two adjacent classes. Adolescent dating activities also differed according to class, ranging from formal dances at the country club limited to members, through high school dances open to all but attended mainly by middle-class students, to the tavern visits and jalopy rides of lower-class youngsters.[18]

Differential dating practices are consistent with the strong tendency of Americans to select marriage partners from the same class. Several investigations have shown that the majority of marriages at all social levels unite class equals. When class lines are crossed the man in most cases selects a partner from a lower class, whereas women marry men from class levels lower than their own much less frequently.[19] This pattern is in accordance with our cultural norms, which approve marriage at one's own level for both men and women but which in some measure also consider "marrying up" a proper channel of social mobility for girls, who are expected to use their attractiveness to make "a good marriage."

Finally, there are significant class differences in family stability. Old, established upper-class families, who are generally part of an extended kinship group, tend to be very stable, which fits in with their generally conservative attitudes and behavior. A sharp contrast exists in the case of new upper-class families, unsupported by kinship traditions and whose members are apt to stress the freedom and initiative of the individual. Lacking the stabilizing influence of the extended family, "lower-upper" families show a higher incidence of divorce and broken homes.[20]

Middle-class families, on the other hand, are generally stable units in comparison with both upper-class families and working-class families, though they are not usually part of a large kinship group. This stability characterizes both the upper and the lower reaches of the middle class: divorce is rare, desertion infrequent, and premature death rates are low.[21]

Instability is much more frequent at the working-class level, where it is partly a by-product of the difficult living conditions to which many working-class families are subjected. In this group, according to recent studies, instability increases as one descends the status ladder. At the upper levels of the working class from a fourth to a third of the families are broken by divorce, desertion, or premature death before the children reach adulthood, while at the lowest status levels 50 to 60 percent of the families with adolescent children have been broken, often more than once.[22] Family instability is even greater, of course, among nonwhites than among whites.

RACIAL, ETHNIC, AND RELIGIOUS DISTINCTIONS AND THE STATUS SYSTEM

A discussion of the status dimension of social stratification in the United States would be incomplete and unrealistic if it took no account of the racial, ethnic, and religious distinctions that complicate the status system. To be sure, these distinctions are aspects of the social structure that may be analyzed separately and are not the direct concern of this study. However, these are distinctions that function as important criteria for the social ranking of individuals and the formation of status groupings in America.

This function is most clearly evident in the exceedingly high barriers by which Negroes, Orientals, and many Mexicans are excluded from intermarriage and intimate social participation with other Americans. In the South legal and unofficial segregation, customary patterns of physical avoidance, and the insistence of deferential behavior on the part of the Negro set Negroes and whites so sharply apart that many observers term this situation a "caste system." Others point to the differences between the caste system of India and the pattern of Southern Negro-white relations and question the applicability of the term *caste*.[23] Terminological niceties, however, do not change the fact that the fundamental rules of the system prevent social relations which imply equality, holding that any white individual is socially superior to any colored person, regardless of differences in education, occupation, or personal characteristics.

The reality of racial barriers shows up dramatically, for example, in the important area of income, where differentials between white and Negro continue and have even increased, despite the rise in living levels and opportunities since the 1940s. Thus in most Northern states in 1959 the average income of Negroes was about 70 percent of the white average, and in the deep South it was well under half the white average. We have already seen from Table II that the distribution of Negroes in occupations is sharply different from that of whites. In 1960 about 40 percent of all jobs held by Negroes were in the categories of laborer or service worker—janitor, porter, cook, and the like. And even in these low-paying jobs Negroes earned much less than whites—for example, 25 percent less in the nonfarm laborer category.[24] It seems clear that such income and occupational differentials are to be explained not only in terms of differences in training and skill levels but also by discrimination per se.

The separation is less extreme in regions of the country where racial segregation is not legally imposed but is nevertheless practiced through various discriminatory devices. The inferior status of the Negro stands in contradiction to the belief in equality of opportunity and the religious values that stress the brotherhood of all men. This incompatibility between the traditional American creed and the practice of discrimination stimulates stress and conflict. In part this contrast also accounts for the continuously shifting patterns of race relations, including change in the South where Negroes are now making rapid progress in gaining the vote and improving their educational and occupational opportunities. Nevertheless, the color line still divides the two races socially into white and Negro worlds sharply insulated from each other.

Improvement in economic position, coupled with the continuance of color segregation, has helped to bring about a separate class structure within the Negro community, which forms the basis of a separate Negro status hierarchy. The growing occupational differentiation of the Negro population, especially in the cities, has led to the emergence of a threefold class structure.[25] To a large extent the Negro class system parallels the white, but largely due to the greater limitation of economic and educational opportunities for Negroes there is no exact correspondence of the classes. The Negro upper class consists of professionals and businessmen whose incomes are about the same as those of the white upper-middle- rather than white upper-class individuals. The Negro middle class is composed mainly of persons whose skilled, semiskilled, and service occupations correspond to working-class status in white society. The bottom of the Negro class structure, the unskilled workers who earn a very precarious living, still comprises about two-thirds of the Negro population, a much larger proportion than the corresponding segment in the white class structure.[26]

Prestige in the Negro community, as in white society, depends not only on occupation, income, and education but also on style of life, respectability, family lineage, and the additional criterion of skin color. As a survival from the days of slavery when a light complexion, the result of race mixture, was a mark of social superiority and often of freedman's status, skin color has remained a determinant of prestige in the Negro status system: the darker the skin the lower the status. However, as economic differentiation develops and income, occupation, and education increase, skin color is declining as an important basis of social status. And most recently, of course, the relationship between skin color and status has come under strong attack from advocates of Black Power and black separatism as well as a number of other less militant groups. A more positive stress upon negroid features has even been taken up by many middle- and upper-class blacks as the Negro has come to redefine his self-conception and to take greater pride in his unique heritage and contributions to American culture.

The castelike exclusion of Negroes and other nonwhite groups from intermarriage and intimate social intercourse with other Americans illustrates the operation of racial distinctions as status factors in their most drastic form. But the status position of Negroes differs essentially in degree, not in kind, from that of other ethnic and religious minorities. During the second half of the nineteenth century and the first decades of the present century successive waves of immigration brought large numbers of peoples to the United States who differed from the "old American" population and from one another in religious, national, and cultural origin. Frequently arriving penniless and illiterate, the members of these ethnic groups were generally forced to begin life in this country at the bottom of the occupational ladder, filling the most menial and poorly paid jobs. Their low-prestige occupations and poverty, their alien languages and "strange" behavior, and sometimes their religion, relegated these ethnic groups to the least desirable residential districts. Hence they were excluded from social intercourse with old Americans, who looked down upon them as inferior "foreigners."

In time the immigrants and their children and grandchildren became acculturated, many of them climbing the job ladder, accumulating wealth, and moving into better residential neighborhoods. As several studies have shown, the rate of upward mobility has varied among the various ethnic groups. Thus those who came early and spoke English, as the Irish, those whose cultural and religious background resembled that of the old Americans, as the Germans, Scandinavians, and other northwestern Europeans, and those who in Europe had practiced urban-commercial occupations, as especially many of the Jews, have advanced rapidly. Other groups, who arrived more recently and who came from cultures differing more sharply from the dominant American pattern, particularly many of the immigrants from southeastern Europe and French Canada, have progressed more slowly.[27]

Status recognition, however, has lagged behind economic success for most ethnic groups. Although at times they have achieved considerable economic and political power, most persons of ethnic origin have been unable to win social acceptance by high-status, old American groups. Several investigations show that membership in an ethnic minority group automatically excludes individuals and families from intimate social participation with top local status groups even though they possess all other requisite "elite" characteristics.[28]

Rebuffed in their attempts to win social acceptance, members of some ethnic groups have developed their own group ways, each with its own status hierarchy which often resembles the old American prestige system. For example, several years ago eight different Junior Leagues for upper-class women were reported in New Haven, Connecticut:

> . . . The top ranking organization is the New Haven Junior League which draws its membership from "Old Yankee" Protestant families whose daughters have been educated in private schools. The Catholic Charity League is next in rank and age—its membership is drawn from Irish-American families. In addition to this organization there are Italian and Polish Junior Leagues within the Catholic division of the society. The Swedish and Danish Junior Leagues are for properly connected young women in these ethnic groups, but they are Protestant. Then, too, the upper-class Jewish families have their Junior League. The Negroes have a Junior League for their top-drawer young women. This principle of parallel structures for a given class level, by religious, ethnic, and racial groups, proliferates throughout the community.[29]

The continued segregation of ethnic communities, however, has been challenged by the "triple melting pot" hypothesis suggested over twenty years ago by Ruby Jo Reeves Kennedy and developed later by Will Herberg.[30] This hypothesis argues that ethnic barriers have been breaking down within the three major religious divisions—Protestant, Catholic, Jewish—and that ethnic groups of the same religion have become more integrated. Yet numerous studies indicate that, whereas this process may hold to some extent for certain white ethnic groups, it has hardly occurred for nonwhites and some other groups. Thus there is little reason to believe that, because Negro Catholics attend mass together with whites, they are integrated in any meaningful way into the white Catholic subculture. The same can be said of the Catholics of Mexican and Spanish descent in the Southwest and the Puerto Ricans of New York City. In sum, ethnicity remains as a segregating influence and status barrier that is often as effective as religion, if not more so.[31]

PRESTIGE AND STRATIFICATION IN THE LOCAL COMMUNITY

In the foregoing sections we have discussed some of the distinctive cultural attributes and behavior patterns that, together with occupation, income, wealth, and education, form the basis of the differential distribution of social prestige in American society. These are the criteria by which Americans rank one another as socially superior, equal, or inferior.

In small communities where the residents are related by personal contacts or at least know one another "by reputation," a reasonably complete and accurate view of the status structure may be obtained by asking a panel of adult residents to rate the "social standing" of all or most local families and individuals. As would be expected, the picture that emerges by using this procedure differs for each community, depending upon its particular history, size, and other features and upon the methods of the researcher. Some community studies thus report from two to six or more discrete status levels, while others describe a prestige continuum "in which the status of families varies by small degrees from those with the greatest prestige to those with the least, with no significant gaps or lines of division recognized by the members of the community."[32]

Although further research is needed to clarify the matter, it seems probable that some of these differences stem from a conceptual confusion of prestige and status groups. *Prestige* refers to a social-psychological system of attitudes in which superiority and inferiority are reciprocally ascribed, while *status groups* are functioning collectivities of persons of similar prestige in one another's eyes who interact with one another in intimate social association. The differential distribution of prestige may in fact take the form of a continuum in a given community, while the status groups in the same community may or may not form a series of discrete levels.

This distinction has particular relevance for the study of the status stratification of large urban communities, where each resident knows only a few of the other inhabitants. It is impossible to delineate here a definite hierarchy of status groups on the basis of mutual ranking or by means of participant observation. Large cities have status structures and their social profiles are marked by typical levels of prestige. But big cities consist of large numbers of individuals and families who possess similar prestige characteristics and who form a complex pattern of coordinate status groups at each level of the prestige hierarchy.

The criteria of prestige differ somewhat between large and small communities. In small communities, especially if they are slow-changing, family lineage and length of residence are often emphasized more strongly than in the comparative anonymity of large cities, where prestige is based more directly on occupation, income, residence, patterns of consumption, and other highly visible status symbols.

Moreover, positions in local status hierarchies cannot be readily equated. Thus an individual who ranks at the top of the prestige scale of a small community may find that he is granted much less deference when he moves to a large city. Nevertheless, considerable uniformity exists throughout the country in the way in which prestige characteristics are evaluated. As a result, prestige claims are frequently transferable from one community to another, especially if the communities are similar in size and broad social characteristics. Transferability of prestige is sometimes matched by transferability of power, which in fact may give its owner prestige wherever he resides. But power and its structure require separate treatment; they are the subject of the following chapter.

VI

The Structure of Power: Class, Formal Authority, and Informal Controls

In a society characterized by marked inequalities in the distribution of income and wealth, fairly closely associated with significant differences in prestige, one would expect to find large differentials of authority and power. This expectation is borne out by the facts: individual Americans differ sharply in their ability to control and manipulate the behavior of others. But it is not easy to present documentary evidence about the unequal distribution of power, partly because universal franchise presents a formal picture of democratic diffusion of power among all. To look behind the outward forms of the political equality of the ballot is a difficult task, for the highly visible formal processes of political democracy effectively screen from public view the informal behavior of the few who are often in a position to make basic decisions.

But no analysis of inequality of power can penetrate very far into the realities of American society without recognition of a fundamental structural principle that is often ignored because it is so obvious or so thoroughly embedded in our ideology. This is the principle of the separation of the state and economic institutions: in the former, the principle of the democratic process of decision-making by publicly responsible and accountable representatives distributes fairly effective power throughout large segments of the population; whereas the latter, by institutional design, represent a high concentration of power in the hands of a relatively small group of decision makers, which constitutes to a significant degree a self-perpetuating oligarchy—to use the words of A. A. Berle, a leading authority in this field.[1] The concept of liberal or capitalist democracy emphasizes this split between the two areas of decision-making and holds that economic decision-making must not be made subject to the democratic process of public accountability. In the past such a view was given some valid justification by the fact that there were very many businesses and corporations, not very large or monopolistic, and owned and controlled by private individuals, along with a relatively uncontrolled market system that could act as a surrogate "democratic" process of economic regulation. It is recognized by many today, however, that such conditions no longer prevail, and a crisis of legitimacy exists for the business executives who would base their control on firm ground.[2] This crisis stems basically from the fact that the fundamental principle underlying the concept of democracy, namely, that the public has a major voice in making those societal decisions that seriously affect its destiny, is seriously challenged by the principle of private and concentrated control of the economy. This is especially so when it is recognized that the shaping of modern industrial society and the destiny of the people within it are largely a matter of economic decision-making. It goes without saying that much of the conflict of recent and contemporary history throughout the world hinges on this issue.

The separation of the state and the economy is a principle which, though carried further in practice in the United States than in any other major country, is not at all completely realized even here. On the one hand, governmental restrictions do put at least some broad limits on the freedom of action of economic decision makers, for example, the antimonopoly and collusion laws. On the other hand, many members or close collaborators of the economic elite (such as lawyers) come to fill the higher governmental positions to a significant extent and hence help to shape public policy. And of course there is a great deal of less formal influence in both directions between the two institutional areas, which scientific research is only partly able to document.

This whole area of study of power elites, of the interplay of power and authority between institutional areas, and of the nature of the basic structure of controls in its public and private aspects is a very large and important field that is difficult to conceptualize and to investigate in depth, and we cannot review most aspects of it here. In the last few decades sociologists have made an important contribution to the field by focusing on the distribution and characteristics of power holders, especially on the level of the community. We turn to a discussion of some of these studies.

POWER AND CONTROL IN AMERICAN COMMUNITIES

Significant empirical data about the exercise of power have been gathered in a number of studies of local communities. In the latter it is easier to discover who makes the decisions and how they are put into effect than it is on the national level. We shall first discuss four such studies that have now become "classics" and a point of departure for later studies. Although these investigations were undertaken in communities that differed widely in size and are located in various parts of the country—one is a Southern metropolis of 500,000 population, another an industrial city of 50,000 inhabitants in Indiana, a third a small Illinois town of 6,000 residents, and the fourth a rural town in upstate New York with 3,000 inhabitants[3]—their findings revealed important similarities in the structure of power relations.

In each of these four communities is a small power elite, a group of persons well known to each other who make the final decisions about local projects and issues, formulate policy, and control local politics directly or indirectly. The power elite consists of prominent business and banking executives, corporation lawyers, and individuals who are independently wealthy. However, not all major businessmen and persons of wealth are members of the local power elite. High economic position or wealth is a prerequisite, giving access to the power groups, but active participation in the group is largely a matter of individual choice. Access to power is not synonymous with its actual exercise.

In Southern Metropolis a group of forty top leaders who can "move things" in the affairs of the community was identified, interviewed, and observed in action. Twenty-three of these power wielders were executives of large manufacturing companies, of banking, finance, and insurance firms, or of major commercial enterprises; five were corporation lawyers; another five were wealthy female "socialites"; four were politicians; two were labor leaders; and one was a dentist. The businessmen represented a large majority of the principal economic interests of the city and were related to one another as directors on boards of local corporate enterprises.[4]

Southern Metropolis' controlling elite is divided into several cliques, the members of which interact among themselves informally and without publicity in formulating policy on community projects. Having made the decisions, they are able to mobilize several hundred lesser leaders who serve on formal committees, boards of agencies, and so on and act as public executors of policy.[5] The power of the top decision makers, however, is not limited to civic enterprises, charity drives, and such economic matters as attracting new industries. They are also able to dominate local and state government.

Although no formal tie-in between the business leaders and the apparatus of government exists, the mayor of Southern Metropolis and the county treasurer, both of whom were successful businessmen themselves before seeking public office, as well as the heads of all governmental departments, are keenly aware of the power of the key businessmen and make no major decision without consulting and "clearing" with the economic leaders.[6] The business executives are thus able to influence the formalized processes of government in their favor. One important member of the group, the president of a large manufacturing company, was known as the power behind the governor of the state—a large campaign contributor, he was reputed to be able to summon the governor to his own office for important conferences.[7]

Using the machinery of local and state government as a convenient instrument for the pursuit of its own goals, the elite group of Southern Metropolis is able to dictate policies effectively in matters involving its economic interests, such as keeping taxes down and holding wages low. The lesser civic leaders, the "executors of policy," may voice some opinions on policy but usually their advice goes unheeded. The bulk of the population exercises little power in the determination of economic, civic, or governmental policies. In recent years, however, organized labor, traditionally excluded from policy decisions, is beginning to make its weight felt, the two top local union officials being increasingly consulted by the other members of the power elite.[8]

The structure of power observed in the 1930s by the Lynds in Middletown,[9] an Indiana city of then about 50,000 population, was strongly dominated by a singly wealthy family of manufacturers—a pattern of concentrated and personalized power which is no longer common in manufacturing cities of this size. This family of five brothers (the "X family"), who came to the city in the 1880s and began to manufacture glass fruit jars, by 1945 had not only expanded their plant to the largest of its kind in the world but also controlled the local credit resources through three family members who served on the board of directors of the only local bank. They also held interests in some of the city's other manufacturing plants, owned Middletown's interconnecting trunk railways, its largest department store, and two dairies, and partially controlled a local brewery and the largest furniture store. They had also invested heavily in real estate helping to create a new fashionable residential section, and they owned a controlling interest in Middletown's morning paper.

On this solid economic foundation the members of this civic-minded family played a major role in practically all areas of Middletown's life. As the Lynds point out, however, this family's pervasively personal system of community control was not the result of conscious, deliberate manipulation.[10] It was rather an informal and largely unplanned and uncoordinated web of control, based on economic position which enabled the "X family" to enjoy prominent roles and to exercise decisive influence in civic and political affairs. But this control was not the automatic by-product of great wealth and economic power, illustrated by the fact that another family of very wealthy manufacturers in Middletown elected to remain inconspicuous and aloof from community affairs.

As in the cases of Southern Metropolis and Middletown, Elmtown, a smaller community of 6,000 persons in upstate Illinois, exhibits a pattern of concentrated power exercised by a few upper-class families who are locally known as "the society class." [11] The heads of these families are engaged in large business or farming enterprises and a few are independent professionals. They own the two banks of the town, its manufacturing plants, almost all the business buildings in town, and extensive farm lands in the surrounding area.

Since large tax bills accompany their extensive ownership, these Elmtown families have a direct interest in keeping assessments and tax rates low and therefore influence public works projects, schools, welfare programs, and other public expenditures which involve tax bills. Their control is exercised largely behind the scenes, through the two major political party organizations and the newspaper, which is owned and published by one of the upper-class families.

The conservative policies advocated by Elmtown's top families are executed by the outwardly prominent and prestigious upper-middle-class civic leaders and by the predominantly lower-middle-class elected and appointed public officials. Representatives of both of these larger groups act as agents for the powerful elite families. Except for a judgeship and the district attorney's post, candidates for public office (at the time of the study) are not themselves members of the upper class. Generally, in the local community upper-class families prefer to control the policy-making processes informally, leaving the outward trappings of power to middle-class persons.

Interesting similarities as well as significant differences in the power structure of a small community are shown in a recent study of a rural upstate New York town described by Arthur J. Vidich and Joseph Bensman.[12] About 3,000 people live in Springdale township, about 1,000 of them in Springdale village; the others live in several hamlets and in the open country. The economy of this community is based primarily on dairy farming and lumbering, while the village functions as a farm trading center.

Local political institutions consist of a village board and a town board. The jurisdiction of the village board includes a variety of village facilities like street lighting, water supply, fire protection, village roads, street signs, and parks. The town board has jurisdiction over the open country that surrounds the village. It keeps the town records and supervises the upkeep of the roads, which is by far its most important function. Village politics is dominated by local businessmen, while the town government is dominated by prosperous farmers. There is a certain amount of latent tension between these two political bodies, but they are united in a firm belief in low taxes, low expenditures, and the reliance on state and federal subsidies—the county in which Springdale is located receives roughly $20.00

in state aid for every $1.00 which it pays in taxes of all kinds.

Actually the elected village and town officials are merely front men for an "invisible government" of four top leaders. The leading figure is the owner of a prosperous farm-supply business. He is assisted by the editor of the local newspaper and the legal counsel of the village board on the village level and by yet another lawyer on the town level. These four leaders have created a political machine. They work behind the scenes and make sure that the town and village government bodies reach the "right" decisions. The elected officials of these boards serve as secondary leaders without real policymaking powers.

The power of the four well-known "invisible" leaders rests primarily on the fact that they are able to provide important connections between Springdale and the state and national power centers. For contrary to the cherished traditional ideology of small town independence and grass roots democracy, this rural town has virtually abdicated all its powers and has surrendered them to the state and national power centers.

> . . . at almost every point . . . the village and town boards adjust their action to either regulations and laws defined by state and federal agencies which claim parallel functions on a statewide or nationwide basis or to the fact that outside agencies have the power to withhold subsidies to local political institutions. . . . Decisions which are made locally tend to consist of approving the requirements of administrative or state laws.[13]

In short, the case of Springdale provides a telling illustration of the way in which rural life in the twentieth century has become dependent on the institutions and dynamics of urban mass society.

Since the Hunter study was published in 1953 a number of other community power studies have been conducted, with a variety of results concerning the nature of local power structures. Thus John Walton, in a survey of community power research conducted in the twelve years following Hunter's study of "Regional City," summarizes the results of thirty-three studies dealing with fifty-five communities.[14] Classifying the types of power structure into four categories, Walton lists eighteen communities with a "pyramidal" or concentrated power structure similar to that found in the four communities reviewed above. Seventeen were found to have a "factional" structure, that is, a pattern consisting of two or more durable factions; fourteen were "coalitional"—made up of fluid coalitions of interest; and five were "amorphous"—lacking any persistent pattern of power.

Although it may well be the case that these varying results accurately reflect the actual structures of power in these communities, there is some suspicion that the results obtained may be a reflection of the particular methods of study used and perhaps also of the theoretical orientations of the researchers. Serious controversy has arisen over the relative merits of two major methods of research on community power. One is referred to as the "reputational technique" and was used by Hunter and a number of other sociologists. In this technique knowledgeable informants in a community are asked to identify those people in the community who are most influential in getting things done. Sometimes a second step is added whereby the initial list of power holders is given to a second group of informants who are asked to sort them further into the most influential leaders. The second technique, the "decision-making" or "issues" approach, is favored by several political scientists and some sociologists. Here the study focuses on particular community issues and seeks to identify the leaders who appear to be active or instrumental in resolving them.

The severest critics of the reputational approach have been a number of political scientists who are skeptical of the existence of a pyramidal power structure in most communities and who favor instead a "pluralist" theory of community power, which envisions a number of competing power or interest groups that continually change in composition and alignment as community issues change.[15] These critics argue that the reputational approach only provides a list of people who have a reputation for power but does not show that these people actually exercise influence over important issues in some monolithic way. Their argument, however, does not rest on an actual test of the reputational approach.

Such a test was reported in 1962 by two sociologists, William V. D'Antonio and Eugene Erickson.[16] They studied six Southwestern and Mexican border communities, utilizing a two-step reputational technique and also an analysis of actual involvement in specific community issues. They concluded that the reputational technique was quite effective in distinguishing those who exercised general community influence as well as those whose influence was related to specific issues. About a dozen persons consistently reappeared on all the informants' lists in a community, although these persons were not construed to make up a single solitary power elite. In the actual decision-making it seems that typically there is a larger group of influentials only a few of whom are involved in any specific issue and a smaller group involved in several or most of the issues.

In sum, it would appear at present that the more detailed nature and operations of community power structures are still an open question, calling for further studies of the various research techniques and the conditions under which each of them might be most fruitful in unraveling the complexities of this area.

IS THERE A NATIONAL POWER STRUCTURE?

If the study of power relations in local communities suggests a fairly consistent pattern of civic and political controls exercised informally and often behind the scenes by small elite groups including many in high economic positions, the picture appears considerably more complex and amorphous on the national level. Here the scene is marked by a bewildering array of hundreds of great business corporations, financial and insurance firms, trade associations, labor unions, farm organizations, consumer associations, special interest groups, and state and federal governmental agencies, all wielding significant amounts of power and all engaged in a continuous effort to influence public opinion in order to shape national policies.[17] In this complex situation it is exceedingly difficult to discern and delineate clearly the outlines of a national power structure.

Nevertheless, several major attempts have been made to analyze the power structure of the United States. They have come to widely divergent results. Perhaps the most famous but also the most controversial analysis has been presented by C. Wright Mills in his widely read book *The Power Elite*.[18] Mills claims that within American society major national power today resides in the economic, the political, and the military domains and that at the pinnacle of each of these domains there has arisen an elite of people occupying its institutional command posts. He further argues that those who occupy the decision-making positions in these crucial institutional areas "may also be conceived as members of a top social stratum, as a set of groups whose members know one another, see one another socially and at business, and so, in making decisions, take one another into account." [19] Mills also contends that below this elite which makes all key decisions—decisions that carry more consequences for more people than ever before in the history of mankind—there exists a middle level of power wielders, among whom he counts the professional politicians. This middle level is in a semiorganized stalemate. At the bottom level there has developed a mass society of people who are utterly devoid of power. The elite keeps the masses quiet by flattery, deception, and entertainment, while its own power is corrupted by the fact that it is not accountable for its decisions to any organized public. He calls the elite's use of power a "higher immorality" whose general acceptance is an essential structural feature of the mass society which America has become in the twentieth century.

As numerous critics have pointed out, Mills' analysis is a complex combination of sharp, well-documented insights intermingled with sweeping generalizations that are not supported by the empirical evidence he himself adduces. His analysis is not only an exposition and explanation of the national power structure but also an indictment, a fiery and sarcastic attack on the competence of the power elite in the exercise of its awesome responsibilities and on the moral legitimation of its position in the social structure.[20]

A much less vitriolic but equally ambitious attempt to delineate the top leadership group of the United States has been made by Floyd Hunter, who applied the same reputational technique he previously employed in his study of Southern Metropolis.[21] Compiling a list of top leaders across the nation, using questionnaires, interviews, and informal polls, Hunter concluded that the major policy decisions are apparently made by several hundred top business executives who can be considered national power leaders. They are the moving powers behind the national business associations, the National Association of Manufacturers, the American Bankers Association, the United States Chamber of Commerce, the Association of American Railroads, and a score of other "big business" associations. The names of the businessmen prominent in national affairs appear repeatedly in the news and on the letterheads of business organizations. They participate frequently in national committee meetings, and they seem to travel a great deal, shuttling back and forth across the country from city to city.

Occupying major executive positions in large economic enterprises, these business leaders are formally associated with each other through overlapping and interlocking corporation directorships. They are informally drawn together through personal friendships and other social ties. They are, of course, members of the power elite groups of the cities in which they reside. Representing different sections of the country and different segments of the economy, to a large extent they share a common economic philosophy and have a similar outlook on major social and political issues. And as we have already pointed out, there is a significant amount of movement in both directions between key political posts and high-level economic positions, on the national as well as state and local levels. Furthermore, the mass media of communication overwhelmingly share and support in many active ways the conservative ideology of the business community and hence help to shape pro-business attitudes among large segments of the population.

But these business leaders do not form a tightly knit clique. Nor is there a continuous policy committee of American business that consistently weighs and formulates overall policy. The leaders' association is loose and sporadic, their efforts being coordinated only as the occasion arises; if a particular industry feels seriously threatened by impending legislation, for example, or if major issues affect whole segments of business, the loosely joined but effective network of liaison and communication swings into action. At such times top executives move about the country, conferring at luncheons and other meetings, hammering out a policy line.[22] The latter is then translated into a flow of propaganda and press releases and into lobbying activities by the national associations.

In turn, the business associations may find it necessary to form alliances with friendly "outside" groups, including farm organizations, professional organizations such as the American Bar Association and the American Medical Association, veterans' groups, and so forth. These groups are frequently ready to support the "educational" and lobbying efforts of business organizations, not only because they largely share their social outlook, but also because they expect and need reciprocal help when their own interests are at stake. Thus, based on their great economic power, their high prestige as central figures of our civilization, and their skill at forming working alliances, American business leaders have long exercised a major, and at times dominant, influence upon our national politics.

It is unrealistic, however, to assume that concentrated economic power always has its way and that our national power structure represents a monolithic pyramid of influence and control flowing from "big business" at its apex down through the "allied groups" in the middle to the unorganized mass of citizens at the bottom of the hierarchy. For one thing, as noted earlier, "business" is not a tightly organized group. Like other interest groups, the national business associations represent a wide diversity of special interests which sometimes clash in open conflict over such specific issues as tariffs, taxation, and price controls. The need to compose internal cleavages and conflicts is often present and imposes considerable obstacles to the cohesion necessary for unified action.

Even more important is the fact that the political power of organized business groups on the national level is much less marked than in the local community. As one observer has aptly phrased it, on the national scene economic power can be converted into political power only at a discount,[23] because in recent decades other national groups, especially organized labor and the so-called farm bloc, have attained sufficient power to defeat policies inimical to their interests and, on occasion, to impose their own will. To be sure, the power of such groups does not equal that of organized business; at present they are essentially veto agencies that can limit the leadership of business rather than effectively substitute their own policies. Yet "New Deal" legislation, to cite an imposing case, illustrates that business groups can be forced on the defensive. Legislation of this type also makes it clear that on the national level economic power and political power, although always closely related, are not identical.

Hunter's study has been criticized for having failed to achieve its stated goal of delineating a single, comprehensive policy-making group in the nation, and the whole conception of a national power structure in the form of a pyramidal model which informs the work of both Mills and Hunter has been attacked as an inadequate model. As in the case of the community power studies discussed in the preceding section, several "pluralist" theories of the national power structure have been advanced. The most extreme idea is undoubtedly David Riesman's early view that the power structure of the United States has become almost completely amorphous.[24] There now exists a balance of veto groups, each able to prevent the others from actions threatening its interests and, within far narrower limits, to start things. These groups in effect neutralize each other. Riesman admits that there are still some veto groups that have more power than others and some individuals who have more power than others. But "the only leaders of national scope left in the United States today are those unorganized and sometimes disorganized unfortunates who have not yet invented their group." [25]

While Riesman's conceptions now seem too simplistic and altogether too undifferentiated to permit a realistic grasp of the complexities of the national power scene, a more sophisticated pluralistic theory has been advanced by Suzanne Keller in her book *Beyond the Ruling Class.*[26] It is her thesis that advanced industrial societies like the United States are characterized by the emergence of *multiple* "strategic elites," which comprise not only political, economic, and military leaders but also moral, cultural, and scientific ones. "Whether or not an elite is counted as strategic does not depend on its specific activities but on the scope of its activities, that is, on how many members of the society it directly impinges upon and in what respects." [27] Keller feels that at the present time one can distinguish in the United States at least ten or eleven strategic elites: besides political, economic, and military she analyzes diplomatic, scientific, educational, and religious elites, as well as leading artists and writers, popular entertainers, film stars, and outstanding athletes who also fulfill functions important enough for the social system to qualify them as strategic elites. She contends that the high degree of specialization among these elites imposes a certain measure of equality among them—at least in the long run.

> In highly industrialized societies . . . power has become less arbitrary and personal and is increasingly shared among various groups and institutions. The differentiation of elites into specialized and partly autonomous entities has shattered the image of a single, homogeneous power center. A "center" still exists, of course, but it is internally divided. . . . Today no single strategic elite has absolute power or priority, none can hold power forever, and none determines the patterns of selection and recruitment for the rest.[28]

The pluralist conceptions of national power are undoubtedly correct in pointing up the increasing significance of a number of elites and the fact that competition and conflict among elites tend to mutually restrict their powers. But, as the English sociologist T. B. Bottomore has recently emphasized, they tend to play down the fact that the recruitment of most members of the various elites is still largely from the upper classes of society.

> . . . In the Western societies the elites stand, for the most part, on one side of the great barrier constituted by class divisions; and so an entirely misleading view of political life is created if we concentrate our attention upon the competition between elites, and fail to examine the conflicts between classes and the ways in which elites are connected with the various social classes.[29]

At any rate, it is certain that our knowledge of the national power structure is still entirely inadequate and that much difficult research remains to be done before we shall be able to fathom this murky but highly important area of our national life with any degree of reliability.

VII

Class Awareness and Class Consciousness

The preceding three chapters have traced the inequalities in income and wealth, in life chances and opportunities, in prestige and social participation, in power and authority, which constitute the main features of the American class structure. Since many of these differences are conspicuous and highly visible, the question arises of how people react psychologically to the objective facts of stratification. We recall Karl Marx's famous observation that it is not the consciousness of men that determines their being, but rather their social being, primarily their relation to the mode of production, that determines their consciousness. How valid is this view today? In our terms, to what extent are persons at different social levels aware of these differences? Do individuals in similar economic positions have similar or common sentiments, attitudes, and ideas? Are they aware of the similarity of their economic interests and do they feel the need to safeguard or promote them through collective action?

Questions of this type, designed to probe the degree and extent of class awareness and class consciousness, raise problems of obvious significance for the understanding of the dynamic aspects of class structure. Class consciousness and awareness of common interests have existed at many times and places and have at times led to organized class action and class struggles that changed whole structures of societies. But class consciousness and class conflict do not follow inevitably or automatically from objective class differentiation. People may share class attributes which differ markedly from those of others without being particularly aware of this cleavage. Moreover, thinking and conduct are not determined merely by objective position in the social order but depend in part upon the way in which people perceive and interpret their social circumstances. Therefore we cannot assume the presence of class awareness and class consciousness but must investigate empirically how Americans evaluate existing class differences.

DIFFERENCES IN CLASS ATTITUDES AND POLITICAL BEHAVIOR

Thanks to the flourishing field of public opinion research, we now possess a large body of data which demonstrate conclusively that people in various occupational and income levels differ significantly in their opinions and attitudes on a wide variety of social and political issues. A number of public opinion surveys, as well as specific studies of class attitudes, reveal definite correlations between opinions and income and occupation.[1] Such differences are greatest concerning issues that obviously and directly affect people's interests. Thus persons at lower income and occupational levels typically hold more "liberal" or "radical" sociopolitical views—favoring government control of business, the extension of governmental welfare activities, strong labor unions, and greater social security—than members of higher occupational and income groups. For example, a question asked in 1945 by Richard Centers of a representative national cross section of the adult white male population inquired whether "the working people" should be given more power and influence in government. By occupational divisions the answers were as follows:[2]

	Percent Agree	*Percent Disagree*	*Percent Don't Know*
Large business	24.1	74.1	1.8
Small business	29.2	63.9	6.9
Professional	31.9	65.3	2.8
Farm owners and managers	35.3	53.6	11.1
White collar	49.7	45.6	4.7
Unskilled manual	54.5	28.6	16.9
Farm tenants and laborers	58.8	23.5	17.7
Skilled manual	59.3	31.5	9.2
Semiskilled manual	65.5	25.3	9.2

The opinions of businessmen and professionals, on the one hand, and those of manual workers, on the other, are shown to correspond closely with their objective self-interests, while white-collar employees were almost evenly divided on this issue. Similar differences have been noted with respect to a large number of questions designed to test politicoeconomic attitudes and beliefs.

In 1952 Herman M. Case reported a replication of Centers' study, testing the relationships between social class and attitudes toward the power of workers, government controls, and conservatism.[3] In almost all cases Centers' findings were confirmed.

There is also convincing evidence that class divisions in attitudes and opinions are translated into political activity and expressed through the ballot. Studies of voting behavior indicate that in recent decades party preferences have been closely related to the occupational and income characteristics of voters.[4] The higher-income groups generally support the traditionally more conservative Republican Party, while lower-income groups fairly consistently prefer the Democrats, the party more sharply identified with reforms and social change. Groups that represent extremes of the economic hierarchy thus furnish much of the consistently loyal party vote. The changing vote is largely contributed by the middle-income groups, who voted overwhelmingly Democratic during the Great Depression but who are more inclined to support the Republican Party in times of prosperity.

Thus Oscar Glantz, in a study in Philadelphia reported in 1958, found that about 90 percent of the big businessmen in his sample voted Republican in the 1948 and 1952 Presidential elections, whereas approximately 80 percent of the working-class respondents voted Democratic.[5] On the basis of responses to a number of questions about economic affairs, he estimated that 63 percent of the business elite were persistently oriented toward business interests and 43 percent of the union workers were persistently oriented toward labor interests. (It is of importance for an understanding of American politics to note that a third of the big businessmen and over half of the workers were "indeterminate" in their orientation.)

A number of later surveys and polls confirm the general tendency for voting behavior to reflect class position, though there has been a good deal of fluctuation in the correlation depending on the salience of other factors such as the personalities of candidates and the political issues under debate.[6] Despite the fluctuations, however, Robert Alford's analysis of data from a large number of surveys conducted from 1936 to 1960 shows no clear decline of class-based voting in the United States.[7]

However, the cleavages along class lines which are evident on questions dealing with the control of economic affairs, the place of labor unions, and political preferences, where people's opinions largely coincide with clearly perceived self-interests, exist side by side with other attitudes which indicate firmly held common values and traditions regardless of class position. Thus many persons in all classes cling to the traditional belief in the existence of wide opportunities to get ahead.

What conclusions can we draw from evidence of this type, which establishes the existence of opposing attitudes on socio-political issues between persons of different class levels but which also shows considerable overlapping in attitudes—substantial minorities on each class level do not share the attitudes of their fellows who are similarly situated—as well as the pervasive strength of the traditional belief in equality of opportunity?

There can be little doubt that Americans are well aware of sharp differences in wealth, power, and prestige and that they are inclined to vote in accordance with their objective interests. Yet at the same time there is a strong tendency to perceive and interpret objective economic differences as *individual,* not *class,* differences. Clinging to the traditional view that the United States is essentially an "open-class" society of extensive opportunity, most Americans seem to consider class differences to be the result of individual abilities. In this view, wealthy and powerful positions are occupied by persons who have the capacities and luck to attain them, while poverty is defined as fundamentally the individual's own responsibility. Even many severely deprived people consider their position as temporary and believe that they, or their children at any rate, have a good chance to climb the social ladder at least a few rungs. Under such circumstances feelings of class loyalty and solidarity do not develop easily.

CLASS IDENTIFICATION AND CLASS CONSCIOUSNESS

The fact that many Americans have vague and hazy ideas about class has been demonstrated by several studies designed to ascertain whether individuals feel that they belong to a specific class. When questions are open-ended, that is, so worded that they do not require the respondent to place himself clearly in a designated class, interviewers find that many people either show little or no class awareness or have considerable doubts about the class to which they belong. Thus a cross section of 200 persons interviewed in Ventura, a California city of about 20,000 population, were asked, "What would you say are the most important *differences* found among the people of Ventura? That is, what different groups or categories would you divide them into?" Only 35 to 40 percent of the replies were couched in terms indicating class or socioeconomic categories. Subsequently further questions specifically related to class were asked, but a quarter to a third of the respondents seemed unfamiliar with or confused by the concept of class.[8]

Quite similarly the pretest of an investigation in Minneapolis, a much larger city, found that when respondents were asked "cold" to what social class they belonged, a large proportion questioned the interviewer as to the meaning of social class.[9] Therefore, a series of general questions about the existence of social classes and their characteristics were utilized before presenting the direct question, "Which one of these classes are you in?" In spite of this preparation, 14 percent of the respondents answered "no class," 20 percent answered "don't know," and 5 percent refused to answer.[10] When the respondents were asked Centers' four-choice question limiting responses to "upper," "middle," "lower," and "working class," 42 percent identified with the working class, and 31 percent with the middle class. But when given three choices, with "working class" eliminated, 76 percent identified with the middle class. It is clear that such class designations are not especially meaningful for many Americans.

Considered in conjunction with the material on attitudes and opinions previously presented, the data on class identification confirm the conclusion that the United States is characterized by a rather low degree of class awareness. The widespread reluctance to recognize or admit the existence of classes and the persistence of the American dream of equality of opportunity require a forced-choice question to induce many, perhaps most,

Americans to identify themselves with their objective class position.

If class awareness is limited, class consciousness in the Marxian sense is even less developed. As C. Wright Mills points out, class consciousness of this kind requires that "there must be (1) a rational awareness and identification with one's own class interests; (2) an awareness of and rejection of other class interests as illegitimate; and (3) an awareness of and a readiness to use collective political means to the collective political end of realizing one's interests."[11] These three conditions exist only in rudimentary form in this country at the present time. There is little of the sharp polarization of attitudes, the irreconcilability of viewpoint, and the internal cohesiveness that set the working class apart from the middle and upper classes in many European countries and lead to intermittent but open class struggle.

Evidence for this lack of sharp polarization is provided by a few recent studies which show, however, that when class consciousness is strong a high degree of polarization of attitudes and political behavior occurs. Thus Glantz, in the investigation mentioned above, found clear class consciousness among only 40 percent of his big businessmen and among only 28 percent of his unionized workers. However, 100 percent of these class-conscious big businessmen voted for the Republican candidates in the 1948 and 1952 Presidential elections, and about 90 percent of the class-conscious union workers voted for the Democrats. The corresponding figures for the nonclass-conscious respondents in both cases were substantially lower. Glantz also confirmed that the motives the class-conscious person offered for voting as he did were class-related.

Alford's analysis of class-based voting in four Anglo-American countries shows substantially higher voting by class in Great Britain and Australia, with the United States third and Canada lowest. Alford suggests that such class voting in this country is so low, but still exists, primarily because, whereas the major political parties are not explicitly linked to class organizations and do not appeal for support on a class basis, many voters *perceive* the parties as representing particular class interests and vote accordingly.[12] In fact, in recent years there has been growing disaffection with both major parties precisely because, in their attempts to find mass support across all lines of cleavage, they avoid debating major issues, many of which involve class interests, *and* thus provide no clear choice to the electorate.

To be sure, some of the elements conducive to the growth of militant class consciousness are present in our society, and there are certain trends which point in that direction. The activities of economic interest groups, discussed in the preceding chapter, are evidence of a growing conviction on the part of large segments of the population that they have common economic and political interests. This recognition is most marked at present among the wealthy and powerful business elite, who come much closer to forming a self-conscious and cohesive class than any other stratum. Middle-class individuals, few of whom belong to large-scale economic organizations, do not especially think of themselves as members of a class, their psychological feelings and political outlook often diverging widely from their economic interests. Powerful labor unions among manual workers indicate some degree of class awareness, but there is little evidence, as we have seen, that American workers picture themselves as a cohesive class set apart from and in opposition to other classes.

STATUS AWARENESS AND PRESTIGE PERSPECTIVES

Class awareness and class consciousness should not be confused with an awareness of prestige rankings. People may differ sharply from others in income, wealth, and life chances and yet be unaware of the similarity of their own economic interests and the need to act collectively to safeguard them. But prestige is a social-psychological category: individuals or groups cannot enjoy it unless their prestige claims are recognized by others who are willing to give them deference. The existence of status differences consequently depends upon awareness of prestige rankings.

As indicated earlier in this study, however, perception of prestige rankings and awareness of the existence of status groups who share similar amounts of prestige differ from one community to another. In small and stable communities the differential distribution of prestige is often sufficiently apparent to permit a fairly precise ranking of all local residents in a definite status hierarchy, while this procedure is inapplicable in complex and rapidly changing large cities. In other words, status awareness is more developed in small communities where prestige differences play an important role in the face-to-face interaction of residents than in the greater anonymity of the large city where prestige distinctions are largely irrelevant in many impersonal contacts.

Perception and awareness of prestige arrangements not only vary from one type of community to another but are affected by the location of people in the status structure. Several community studies indicate that local status arrangements are conceived quite differently by individuals on different levels of the prestige hierarchy. Members of the top-ranking local status groups, who "look down" upon all other members of the community, generally see the whole community as divided into definite prestige groups, differentiating precisely between the various levels. Those near the middle of the prestige order usually do not discriminate as finely between "new" and "old" upper-class groups as do the top groups themselves, while lower-class people frequently lump all of the upper and upper-middle status groups together. Having little personal contact with higher-status people, lower-class individuals show a vague conception of the intricate prestige differentiations that are matters of importance to the higher-status groups. Members of the lower class are inclined to equate prestige with wealth and power in rather simple fashion and to perceive prestige differences as individual differences, not as a system of status groups.[13]

CLASS CONSCIOUSNESS AND THE AMERICAN DREAM

The coexistence of sharp class differences and the conspicuous lack of corporate or militant class consciousness, which is one of the most important contrasts between American and European systems of stratification, calls for some explanation. The persistence of the idea of classlessness and the belief in extensive opportunity in the face of objective class differences and marked inequalities constitute one of the most intriguing problems of sociological analysis. The lack of militant class consciousness in this country is the result of the interplay of several factors.

One of these factors forms part of the historical heritage of this nation. The absence of a feudal past and of a hereditary aristocracy stimulated the development of a widespread acceptance of "democratic" social manners throughout all levels of American society. The meticulous use of honorific titles so common in many European countries is considered absurd in the United States where stiff formality is frowned upon, and even men in highly prestigious positions are expected to be "folksy" and "common like an old shoe" in personal contacts. To be sure, this equalitarianism of manners is superficial but it effectively mitigates and disguises psychological feelings of social distance and inhibits the crystallization of polarized class sentiments.

The outward appearance of social equality is strengthened by the high standard of living and the competitive pattern of consumption. For one thing, American capitalism has produced a high level of material comfort for the majority of the population, including large segments of the working class. The result is that most people feel that they have a stake in the existing system: their dissatisfactions and frustrations are channeled into competitive aspirations and their energies are directed toward getting more of the comforts rather than a critique of the system that produces them.

Moreover, the mass production of consumers' goods lends the whole economic system a pervasive illusion of equality. The pattern of consumption is continuous rather than polarized.[14] The boss may own a Cadillac whereas the worker's car may be a second-hand Chevrolet, but this gap does not *appear* as wide to the American worker as it does to his European counterpart who can afford only a bicycle. And the American worker's wife who may be wearing the ten-dollar copy of the Parisian dress owned by the boss's wife is still modishly clad and might envy but will hardly hate the more fortunate woman. The mass-produced imitation of luxury items (note the striking case of costume jewelry) thus enables members of all classes to imitate the style of life of the higher-prestige groups, and the system of installment buying facilitates even the acquisition of expensive items like automobiles, furniture, and electrical appliances. Unlike Europe, therefore, the rich are much less clearly set off from the poor by visible symbols of material comfort, and almost all groups are motivated by competitive values rather than divided by the unbridgeable chasm that separates the "bourgeoisie" from the "proletariat" in many European countries.

Equalitarian manners and a high standard of living, then, hamper the development of class consciousness because to some extent they function to unite all classes. A situation of a different kind has had a similar influence, although it divides rather than unites the population. This is the system of racial, ethnic, and religious cleavages which serves to insulate socially large numbers of the same class and thereby to blur potential class solidarity. For example, racial, ethnic, regional, and religious group identification and loyalties have greatly retarded the development of a unified labor movement in this country; they no doubt continue to inhibit the growth of class solidarity. Similarly, as long as individuals vote for or against candidates on the basis of race, nationality, religion, or geographical origin rather than on the basis of their economic principles or class background, these ingroup loyalties override potential class loyalties.

But the most important factor inhibiting the development of class consciousness and perpetuating the dream of opportunity, we believe, is the persistence of high social mobility itself, which keeps the class structure fluid and sustains hopes of "getting ahead." The traditional conviction that individuals have a chance to move up the social ladder if they are able, persistent, or lucky, supported by concrete illustrations of this process, most effectively discourages the growth of corporate or militant class consciousness. To be sure, this American dream is bolstered and exaggerated by the ubiquitous and skillful publicity given to exceptional and spectacular cases of individual mobility. But a dream does not persist for a long time unless it is reinforced by some experience.[15] What American does not know of individual cases of conspicuous upward mobility from first-hand observation?

Indeed, social mobility is of fundamental importance in accounting for the domination of competitive attitudes and sentiments over militant class consciousness. More than this, the understanding of the nature of the American class structure as a whole requires study of this crucial phenomenon, social mobility, the subject of the following chapter.

Send for
Mark Kesselman's
book

add
dimensions

Involvement with
national + Fed party
units

national bureaucracy

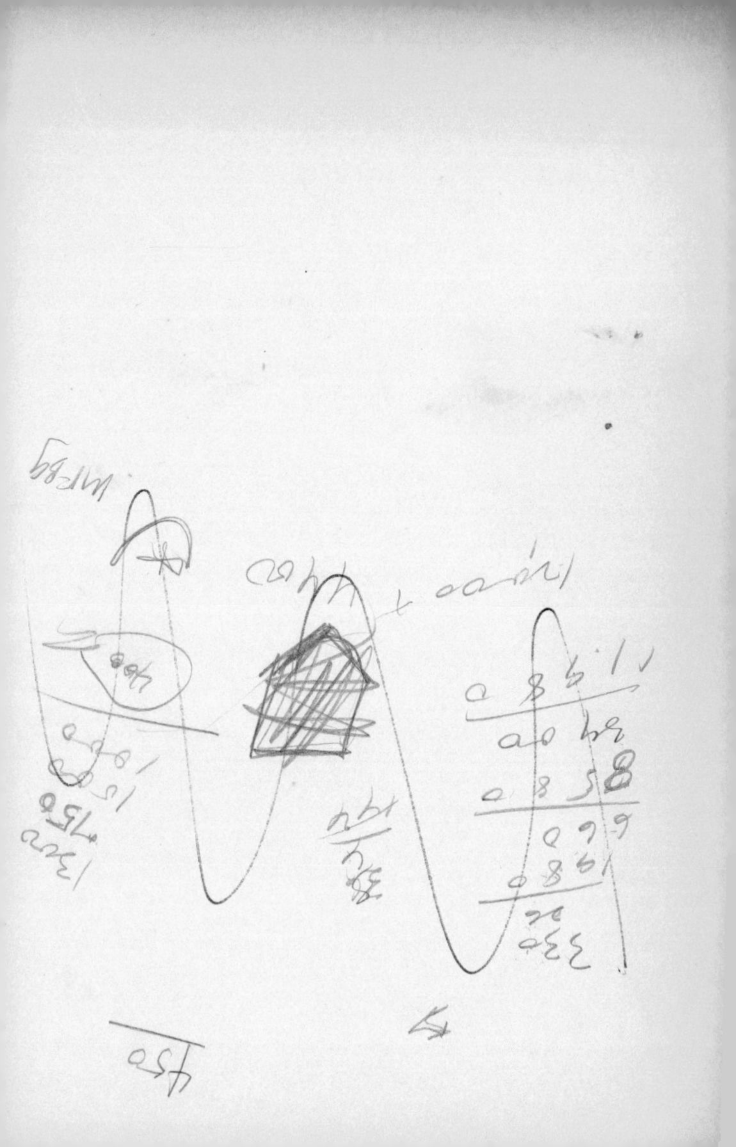

VIII

Social Mobility

One of the most striking aspects of American society is the large degree of fluidity and flexibility of the class system. As we pointed out earlier, most modern class systems are open in the sense that no legal barriers and formal prohibitions prevent the movement of individuals and families up and down the class, status, and power hierarchies. But from its inception the United States has placed greater emphasis on social mobility than any other large nation in modern times. Americans have firmly proclaimed the idea of equality and freedom of achievement and have acclaimed the large numbers of individuals who have risen from humble origins to positions of prominence and affluence. Indeed, the belief in opportunity is so strongly entrenched in the culture that perhaps most Americans feel not only that each individual has the "right to succeed" but that it is his duty to do so. Thus we are apt to look with disapproval upon those who fail or make no attempt to "better themselves."

Our society has of course never been as open as these beliefs proclaim. In Chapter IV we discussed some of the marked inequalities of the class system which greatly reduce the social opportunities of many individuals. Recently a number of investigations have been undertaken to measure the amount of social mobility and to ascertain the extent to which there is continuity and inheritance of class position in the United States.

OCCUPATIONAL MOBILITY

Most attempts to measure social mobility have employed occupational mobility, or movement from one broad occupational group to another, as the principal index of social mobility. This procedure appears justifiable for two reasons: occupational status is closely related to amount and source of income, to education, and to prestige and authority; and occupational information is more precise and more available than other relevant data. It should be kept in mind, however, that movement from occupation to occupation indicates changes in class position more directly than it reflects mobility up or down in either the prestige or the power hierarchy, about which very little quantitative information exists.

Occupational mobility is usually measured in one of two ways. By comparing the occupations of sons with those of their fathers the researcher can ascertain how many people have moved up or down and how many have remained on the same occupational level as their fathers, thus obtaining a measure of intergenerational mobility or continuity. Or the occupational careers of individuals can be traced in order to determine whether they have moved up or down the social ladder. Both of these measures have been employed in several studies.

Although these studies employ different types of samples—some examine a cross section of the nation's male white population,[1] while others focus upon the populations of specific communities[2]—their findings concerning mobility are quite consistent.

The intergenerational comparisons indicate that a high degree of occupational mobility exists side by side with considerable occupational continuity or immobility. The various studies show that about 70 percent of the sons are engaged in occupations different from those followed by their fathers. Occupational change as such is thus much greater than occupational continuity. But a son is more likely to enter his father's occupation than any other single occupation. More sons are employed in the same type of occupation as their fathers' than in any other single occupational group, though the majority of them have moved out of the father's occupation. (The several thousands of specific occupations are grouped under five or six broad occupation categories, for example, "white collar" and "professional," each representing a "level" of occupational prestige.)

However, most of the mobile sons who have left the father's level have not gone very far up or down the occupational hierarchy. Although sons of fathers in a given occupational group can be found at all of the other occupational levels, most of the movement is one step up or down the ladder. Mobile sons of semiskilled workers are thus most apt to become either skilled workers, if they move up, or unskilled laborers if they move down; relatively few of them will rise into the ranks of major business executives or become professionals. The same is true of the other categories, most of the vertical movement being from one level to the next. Moves from the bottom of the scale to the top or the reverse are quite rare. Over two-thirds of the sons work at occupations on the same level or one immediately adjacent to that of their fathers. Therefore, although the amount of mobility is great, it is quite limited in extent.

Nevertheless, on the whole there is more upward than downward mobility. The proportion of sons who move upward from the fathers' level is somewhat greater than those who move downward. Thus one study reports that, of 735 men interviewed in Minneapolis, 26 percent were in occupations on a lower level than their fathers, 30 percent were on the same level, while

44 percent had risen above the parental level.[3] This case seems fairly typical of the overall net upward movement.

These studies also underscore the fact that the rate of intergenerational mobility is higher within nonmanual occupations, on the one hand, and within manual occupations, on the other, than the interchange between these two major groups. The chief barrier to both upward and downward mobility lies between manual and nonmanual occupations, between blue-collar and white-collar jobs. This is the widest gap in the American class structure. Thus, three studies of mobility across the manual-nonmanual line based on national samples compared the occupations of men in the urban labor force with those of their fathers and agree rather closely in their results: Richard Centers' 1945 study found 17 percent upwardly mobile, 8 percent downwardly mobile, and 75 percent stationary; a National Opinion Research Center study of 1947 reported 21 percent, 11 percent, and 68 percent, respectively; and data from a Michigan Survey Research Center study of 1952 reported 19 percent, 13 percent, and 67 percent, respectively.[4] Yet the white-blue collar barrier is by no means insurmountable. A 1949 survey of wage earners in Oakland, California, indicates that of the sons whose fathers were in the nonmanual occupations, 32 percent became manual workers, while of the sons whose fathers were workers, no less than 47 percent moved into nonmanual occupations.[5] This locality, however, was undergoing very rapid growth.

These figures show that proportionately more individuals have moved from the manual into the nonmanual category than the reverse. To be sure, workers' sons moving along this path are most likely to become clerical employees, salesmen, and small business proprietors. Yet however modest the movement may be, the fact that sizable proportions of manual workers' sons do succeed in moving into nonmanual jobs tends to validate and sustain the traditional American dream.

The studies dealing with mobility experienced by individuals during their own occupational careers largely confirm the findings of intergenerational comparisons.[6] They show a wide variety of job experiences, the individual often changing his occupation four or five times during his (still unfinished) working career. However, about half of these shifts in occupation take place within the same broad occupational level, presumably involving neither gain nor loss in social status; while those changes that evidence clear-cut vertical movement are quite limited in range. As in the case of intergenerational mobility, the large majority of all occupational changes within an individual's career result in either maintaining his occupational-prestige level or shifting one step above or below it. Moves from the bottom to the top or the reverse are exceptional, and shifts across the gap between manual and nonmanual work are less frequent than changes within either of these categories. One of these studies reports the manner in which this gap is crossed, indicating that most manual workers who move into white-collar occupations start their own small business or become salesmen.[7] These are the main white-collar employments open to persons with limited education, and here the economic rewards are frequently no higher than those of manual occupations. Nevertheless, the moves of individuals show a slight but definite upward trend.[8]

Finally it should be noted that studies of the social origins of the elite or upper-class groups show a very high degree of occupational inheritance at that level. Thus an early investigation of top business leaders reported by F. W. Taussig and C. S. Joslyn in 1932 assessed occupational movement between grandfathers and fathers and between the fathers and their sons.[9] Of the grandfathers who were major business executives, 79 percent of their sons became major business executives also. The comparable figure for grandfathers who were owners of large businesses was 51 percent inheritance. Inheritance between the father and son generation was similar. About 57 percent of the sons in Taussig and Joslyn's sample had fathers who also were business owners or executives. This contrasts with 10 percent whose fathers were manual workers. In general, it was shown that the business and professional groups, which made up 10 percent of the American population, contributed 70 percent of the business leaders among the sons.

A study by W. Lloyd Warner and James C. Abegglen made

about twenty-five years later continued to show a great amount of upper-class occupational inheritance.[10] A large number of questionnaires was sent to business leaders selected from the 1952 edition of Poor's *Register of Directors and Executives,* representing the highest positions in the largest firms in all types of American business and industry. It was found that 66 percent of the sample had fathers who were business executives (26 percent), business owners (26 percent), or professionals (14 percent). In contrast, 4.5 percent of the fathers were unskilled or semiskilled workers, 10.3 percent were skilled workers, and 8 percent were white-collar workers. Other studies of the business elite have shown similar results.[11] In addition a number of investigations of the social origins of other types of elites—political, military, scientific, and the like—show that the bulk of such elites derive from middle- or upper-class homes.[12]

In summary, the data allow us to draw the following conclusions about occupational mobility during this century: Occupational inheritance characterizes the largest amount of movement between generations. It can be said that the majority of sons end up in occupations at the same or similar class level as their fathers. Nevertheless, there is a good deal of upward mobility, though short in distance, and a somewhat lesser amount of downward mobility, mostly of small degree. Extensive movement is rare: the office-boy-to-president career is highly exceptional. A small precentage of sons of manual workers or farmers, however, have been able to move into white-collar, professional, and even elite positions of one kind or another. Finally the evidence suggests that there has been no significant increase or decrease in the amount of mobility during the century. A large percentage of the mobility that has occurred can be attributed to the continually expanding opportunity structure at the middle and upper end of the occupational scale rather than to increasing equality of opportunity. This limited but fairly widespread mobility (rather than the exceptional, if widely advertised, spectacular career of the self-made man) is characteristic of the contemporary American class system, giving it elasticity and an objective basis for individual aspirations.

STATUS MOBILITY

Although many attempts have been made to measure occupational mobility, we have as yet very little precise information about the amount and extent of status mobility, the process by which persons move up or down the scale of social prestige. In a general way we know, of course, that considerable status mobility exists in our society since prestige is closely related to occupation, income, and wealth. Occupationally mobile persons are likely sooner or later to change their intimate group associations and to participate in new formal and informal organizations. The two processes, however, are by no means identical. Superior occupation, high income, and a good education, to be sure, are prerequisites of high status, but they must be transformed into appropriate behavior and "correct" prestige symbols in order to win the approval and acceptance of high-status groups, a process which sometimes requires more than one generation.

A few case studies describing individual careers of upward and downward status mobility in local communities can be found in sociological literature,[13] and many novels contain interesting fictional accounts of this phenomenon,[14] but to date only one investigation has attempted to analyze the process systematically.[15] This study of the two highest social-status groups of an upstate New York town of 50,000 population concluded that no less than 44 percent of the members of the highest and 50 percent of the members of the next highest status group had themselves been upward or downward mobile.[16] The preponderance of these cases represent upward mobility, and most of them were newcomers to the community who had "the proper credentials": their business or professional connections brought them into contact with the local high-status groups and their cultural attributes and personal traits were acceptable enough "to take them in." [17] Long-time residents found it much harder to win social acceptance by the local elite if they were not born into it. But once lofty social position had been reached, it was not easily lost again. The rule was "once in, always in," and even considerable individual deviations from ingroup standards of behavior were viewed with tolerance.[18]

We should not of course draw general conclusions from a single exploratory study, but the considerable influx into an elite status group of a fairly old town appears significant. Moreover, the finding that newcomers to town encounter less resistance to social acceptability than long-time local residents confirms the widespread popular belief that individuals who were born on the "wrong side of the tracks," if socially ambitious, should move to different communities where their "lowly" social antecedents are not so well known. Such residential shifts are a conspicuous feature of our physically mobile society.

THE ENCOURAGEMENT AND RESTRAINT OF SOCIAL MOBILITY [19]

We have discussed the existence of a large amount of social mobility side by side with considerable continuity and inheritance of social position. Individual opportunities to get ahead are neither as unlimited nor as universal as our tradition proclaims, yet the actual possibilities of acquiring greater income and higher prestige are widespread and real enough to permit a substantial proportion of the population to realize a somewhat modified version of the American dream and to sustain this important phase of our cultural heritage.

The coexistence of flexibility and rigidity invites explanation. The fact that overall social mobility is high and that its net balance is upward is the consequence of several circumstances. Among the latter, technological progress and economic development have played a major role. Within about eighty years the economy has undergone a profound transformation: a predominately agrarian society as late as 1870, the United States has rapidly become a leading industrial nation of the world. These fundamental changes in our economy have brought about major shifts in the occupational structure. As American society has become increasingly industrialized, the proportion of the population engaged in agriculture has greatly declined while the proportion working in the production and distribution of industrial goods and services has correspondingly increased. Moreover, as technological progress during the last few decades has continuously raised physical productivity, the percentage of the labor force required to produce industrial goods has remained comparatively constant while the need of transporting and distributing the ever-growing volume of goods has required that more and more persons work at jobs that provide business and professional services.

Table IX illustrates these developments over a period of fifty years. It shows the precipitate decline of farm owners and farm laborers from 31 percent of the working population in 1910 to 6 percent in 1960 and the corresponding rise of the white-collar occupations from 21 to 40 percent. The increase is especially pronounced among the clerical workers and professionals. The manual occupations expanded only slightly during this period, but it is noteworthy that the proportion of unskilled workers has declined from 21.5 percent in 1910 to 16.4 percent in 1960 while the proportion of semiskilled and skilled workers has increased. These occupational shifts indicate that a large amount of upward social mobility has been brought about by the technological advances and the expansion of the American economy.

This process has been accelerated by the differential birth rate. As we pointed out in Chapter V, for many decades the upper and middle classes have had fewer children than the lower classes. Indeed, for some time the fertility of the higher occupational groups was insufficient to reproduce their numbers from one generation to the next. This situation has created a social vacuum, filled by some of the more numerous children born to farmers and working-class families. In recent years these fertility differentials appear to be lessening, but the contrast between families of manual and nonmanual workers still persists in large measure.

Upward mobility has also been bolstered by the effects of large-

TABLE IX Distribution of Working Population by Major Occupation Groups 1910–1960

Occupation	Percent of Working Population					
	1960	*1950*	*1940*	*1930*	*1920*	*1910*
Farm						
Farmers (owners and tenants)	3.7%	7.3%	10.1%	12.4%	15.5%	16.5%
Farm laborers	2.3	4.3	7.1	8.6	9.4	14.5
Total	6.0	11.6	17.2	21.0	24.9	31.0
White Collar						
Professional persons	10.8	8.5	6.5	6.1	5.0	4.4
Proprietors, managers, officials	8.1	8.6	7.7	7.5	6.8	6.5
Clerks and kindred workers	21.2	18.9	17.2	16.3	13.8	10.2
Total	40.1	36.0	31.4	29.9	25.6	21.1
Manual						
Skilled workers and foremen	13.6	13.8	11.7	12.9	13.5	11.7
Semiskilled workers	18.9	19.8	21.0	16.4	16.1	14.7
Unskilled workers	16.4	16.5	18.8	19.8	20.0	21.5
Total	48.9	50.1	51.5	49.1	49.6	47.9
Total percent	100.0*	100.0†	100.0	100.0	100.0	100.0

* Includes 5.1 percent "occupation not reported."
† Includes 2.3 percent "occupation not reported."

SOURCE: *Statistical Abstract of the United States* (Washington, D.C.: Government Printing Office, 1951), Table 220, p. 188, and (1967), Table 330, p. 232; and *U.S. Census of Population* (1950), Vol. II, Part 1, Table 53, p. 1–101.

scale immigration. Most of the millions of immigrants who came to this country from Europe between the 1880s and World War I were peasants or unskilled workers who spoke no English and entered the American labor market at the bottom level. Many native-born workers were thus "pushed up" one or two steps on the occupational ladder. The restrictive immigration laws enacted since the early 1920s have severely curtailed this European immigration but they have left the doors open to a fairly heavy influx from the Western hemisphere. French-Canadians, Mexicans, and Puerto Ricans have partly replaced the unskilled European immigrants at the lower occupational levels, this inflow being supplemented by internal migrations of Negroes from the rural areas of the South.

Most of these newcomers to industry who hold the bottom jobs belong to racial minority groups that face serious job discrimination. The twenty-one million Negroes, together with an estimated three and a half million Mexicans and one and a half million Puerto Ricans, form a submerged eighth of the nation for whom upward mobility does not operate to the same extent or with as much speed as for the native white population. Several studies of occupational mobility provide extensive evidence that Negroes have a disproportionately large share of the unskilled, dirty, and badly paid jobs and also confirm statistically that the chances of their sons to move out of these unrewarding positions are only a fraction of those of white sons of unskilled fathers.[20] Thus it may be claimed that there are two working classes in the United States today: a white one with relatively ample opportunities for upward mobility; and a Negro-Mexican-Puerto Rican working class which is socially insulated and forms a kind of a lower-caste working base that facilitates the upward careers of whites, especially those who are native-born.

The inferior economic opportunities of racial minority groups, which are also experienced, though to a smaller extent, by southern and Eastern European immigrants and their descendants, constitute one of the major factors that restrain mobility and introduce rigidity into the class structure.

Another sizable obstacle to social mobility is the unequal distribution of educational opportunities. In Chapter IV we emphasized that the amount of formal education significantly influences the individual's class and status position and that the opportunities of working-class children to receive good schooling, especially college education, are still much more limited than those of the children of white-collar families.

These conditions point up the fact that, since education has become a principal aid to upward mobility, educational barriers that confront working-class children guarantee a considerable degree of continuity and immobility in our social structure.

SOCIAL MOBILITY AND SOCIAL CHANGE: STRATIFICATION TRENDS IN THE UNITED STATES

Mounting information about social mobility patterns and the inequalities of life chances and opportunities has encouraged several sociologists to speculate about long-range stratification trends and possible future developments.[21] They have posed a weighty question in various terms: Is America still the land of opportunity? Is social mobility slowing down and the class structure becoming more rigid? Are we heading toward a closed or frozen class system? We do not have sufficient data to answer these queries or to draw final conclusions about stratification trends in the United States. Based on the available evidence, however, a few tentative statements can be made.

The studies of occupational mobility provide no proof that the class structure has become either more or less rigid in recent years. Unless one takes the unwarranted view of the American past as a classless society of equal opportunity as the backdrop against which contemporary reality is to be measured, the available data do not support the conclusion that there is less social mobility today than at any earlier period. Nor can we be certain that there is more upward mobility now than formerly, although one large-scale investigation, by Natalie Rogoff, points in this direction.[22] Her study of the population of Indianapolis not only presents a rigorous comparison of intergenerational occupational mobility in the same community at two different periods, 1905–1912 and 1938–1941, but also distinguishes between mobility caused by changes in the occupational structure itself and mobility independent of this factor. Rogoff concludes that, apart from structural changes, the overall mobility rates were about the same in both periods. However, since considerable changes had occurred in the occupational distribution of the population from 1910 to 1940, leading to a decline in the number of low-status occupations and an increase of high-status occupations, many more sons had moved into occupations higher than those of their fathers in the later period than had been able to do so in the earlier years. In other words, the total amount of vertical mobility had increased between 1910 and 1940.

Moreover, social mobility, or the extent to which individuals are able to move between the various levels of the social pyramid, is only one important measure of its fluidity or rigidity. We also need to consider changes that have occurred in the shape and structure of the social pyramid itself. Figure 3, which is based on the data shown in Table IX, illustrates one aspect of the important changes the class structure has undergone during the last forty years. It shows that the unskilled, low-status occupations which form the basis of the class pyramid have decreased while the higher-status occupations have increased. The most pronounced expansion has occurred in the middle ranges of the scale.

A very similar picture emerges when we consider the changes that have occurred in the distribution of family income between 1929 and 1962. Expressed in 1962 dollars, the proportion of families receiving less than $3,000 annually dropped sharply from 51 percent to 28 percent. The proportion receiving between $3,000 and $6,000 declined slightly from 34 percent to 29 percent. On the other hand, the proportion of families receiving between $6,000 and $10,000 increased from 10 percent to 28 percent, and for those receiving over $10,000 the increase was even sharper, from 5 percent to 15 percent.[23] These figures, it should be noted, reflect not only the greater full-time employment of the major breadwinners but the great increase in the proportion of wives who are employed and hence supplement the total family income.

These shifts in the occupational structure and distribution of income that have occurred during the first half of the twentieth century reflect highly significant transformations of the class

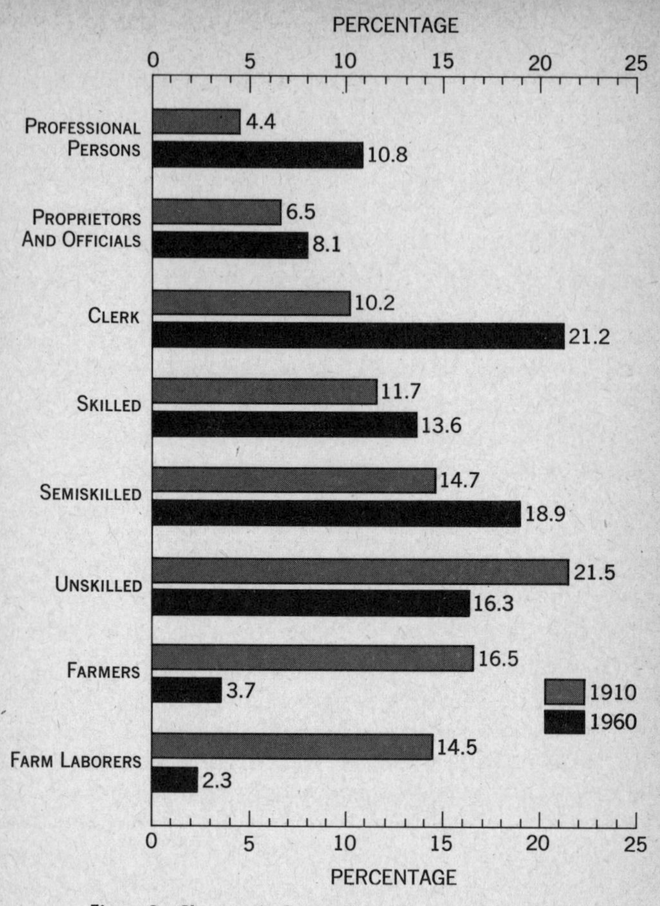

Figure 3 Changes in Occupational Structure, 1910–1960

SOURCE: *Statistical Abstract of the United States* (Washington, D.C.: Government Printing Office, 1951), Table 220, p. 188, and (1967), p. 232.

structure. If the same trends were to continue for another few decades, the lower classes, as currently defined, would gradually disappear and our society might in fact come to approximate the well-known cliché that "America is middle class."

The present outlook, however, is much less optimistic than it was merely a few years ago. This is due to two main factors. First, even if we accept the disputed view that an "income revolution" has been occurring in this century, recent data strongly suggest that it came to an end over twenty years ago. Second, the dramatic and widely publicized "rediscovery" of the poor in the 1960s, largely initiated by Michael Harrington's *The Other America,* and the consequent failure so far of the government's "war on poverty" to make significant inroads into the problem, have considerably dampened earlier optimism.

The view of an income revolution was based on the assumption that, not only had the *amount* of income of the lower groups increased but that their *share* of total income had increased relative to higher groups, so that a true leveling or equalizing process was occurring. We have seen in Chapter IV, however, that changes in income shares took place mainly between different upper groups and affected the lower groups very little or not at all. Data since the end of World War II now show a very stable distribution of shares up to the present, and if there is any trend at all, it appears to be a reverse of the income revolution.[24] The question thus arises, why worry about the distribution of shares of income so long as the amount has increased substantially for the lower groups? The answer to this question may be given in terms of the important concept of "relative deprivation." Beyond a very minimum level, "deprivation" must be defined relative to a number of changing social and psychological factors. A person's expectations, hopes, and fears are a function of his experiences with relation to the circumstances of other individuals and groups in the environment and of his definition of what is possible. The increasing demands of Negroes for justice and equality are a serious case in point. Rising expectations developing out of increased attention to their problems, especially since the 1954 Supreme Court decision rejecting the principle of segregation, have led in turn to a drastic revision of the self-definitions of blacks relative to whites and to a new definition of what is technically possible in the modern era. Though Negroes, as a group, may be better off economically than they were a generation or so ago, their feelings of deprivation, along with their expectations, have increased to the boiling point. This has been a common phenomenon throughout history. Apart from any objectively defined level of living, the fact of inequality—when subjectively defined as such by a group—has been a potent force in social change.

The official recognition in the past few years that roughly 20 percent of the population is living in poverty is only partially offset by the knowledge that the proportion was substantially higher a generation ago. It is not simply that 40 million poor represent a huge population or that it is widely known that there are no technical or inherent economic reasons why this number should not be zero in our affluent and highly productive society. Much of the pessimism in recent discussions of trends in the near future derives from the feeling that the 20 percent poverty figure represents a minimum below which we cannot go without significant changes in the current politicoeconomic framework of power and decision-making. That is, a number of the factors underlying this level of poverty appear to be "hard-core" structural problems that will not be resolved by automatic market mechanisms but rather call for political decisions implying a basic change in social philosophy. Thus unemployment has remained relatively high for the last decade. Behind this situation, in part, lies a long-term decline in the demand for unskilled workers. Displacement by machines is a continuing threat to this class of workers, and computerized automation is an increasing threat to more highly skilled manual workers and white-collar workers as well. What is advocated by some, then, is the need for a large-scale program of education and training for the unskilled and retraining for those displaced by machine and computer. In addition the largest blocks of the poor are made up of the aged, who must make do with minimal pensions; broken families, where wives with young children are unable to work full time; and minority groups—mainly Negroes—who are subject to prejudice and discrimination on the job market as well as elsewhere. The problems of these groups cannot be defined in purely economic terms but constitute complex societal maladjustments whose adequate treatment calls for political decisions that transcend our current "welfare state" philosophy. Indications of the emergence of such a new set of social principles include the current serious discussion of the concept of the guaranteed annual wage, the official governmental pronouncements of the right of all to an adequate job, and the wide attention given to the notion of "the triple revolution."

Our discussion of stratification trends has been couched primarily in terms of social class and the economic dimension. The student using this book, however, has been alerted to the importance also of the other major dimensions, those of status and power. Important changes have also been occurring in these areas that have only begun to be documented. The disaffection of large numbers of intellectuals from governmental policies and the increasing activism of student and Negro groups strongly argue that status considerations and power struggles, though usually with economic overtones, will be major factors accompanying stratification changes in the future.

It is not merely the distribution of material factors that is now under severe criticism, but the whole quality of life generated by a society heavily committed to technical and commercial—rather than social and cultural—development under the protective umbrella of an aggressive military posture and the most powerful and far flung military establishment of any country in history. In historical perspective, as recent studies show,[25] this international commercial-technical-military empire has developed in a quite self-conscious and consensual way in the last few generations by the higher political and industrial decision centers of society. Such a development up to its current extreme dimensions is not unrelated to the facts of social stratification that we have studied. As we have seen in this chapter, the highest degree of social inheritance of position has always occurred at the top of the hierarchy of wealth, status, and power. The men in the highest political and economic decision centers have always represented overwhelmingly the social, cultural, and economic attitudes and values of the few percent of the population who own and control the major wealth and productive apparatus of American society. Thus the major cabinet positions in the federal government are filled by financial and industrial leaders, and major ambassadorial posts by members of families of long–standing wealth and prestige. It is not possible to fully understand the allocation of public moneys in the national budget between domestic needs such as poverty and urban blight, and foreign policy decisions, or to see the "cold war" itself in full perspective, without appreciating the social and economic values of this group of national leaders and the ramifying structure of interpersonal influence and institutional controls that they dominate as a matter of everyday social life. The reactions of increasingly inordinate fear and denial to the successes of the several socialist or communist revolutions, starting with Russia at the end of the first World War, are understandable reactions to a new form of economic institution that is perceived as threatening to the institutional arrangements underlying the positions of the upper groups. That the particular political forms of other societies are of secondary concern to them is easily attested to by a comparison of the strong military response taken toward socialist regimes and the acquiescence and even support accorded to military dictatorships or fascist regimes. The very high correlation in this regard makes it clear that it is the issue of economic democracy and not political autocracy that is perceived as the focal threat both abroad and at home.

Considerations such as the above pose important sociological questions that the student of social stratification has now been forced to study more seriously due to the recent appearance of the most widespread and insistent public critique of Western institutions by the intellectual community that the United States has ever directly experienced. The issues underlying this critique are complex and cannot, of course, be embraced by stratification analysis alone. But it would be as absurd to blink the crucial role of class factors as to accept a simple class conflict theory. The issues have been avoided in great part in academic discussions of stratification, which have focused primarily on such matters as the changing characteristics of the lower classes, the great expansion of the middle class, and the increasing (material) standard of living of all groups. The new student of stratification, however, will find that his studies of wealth, prestige, and politicoeconomic control within the upper 1 percent of the population will also provide a background of data and theory essential to a more informed discussion and critique of the direction of his society's national and international drift.

Notes

Chapter I Social Differentiation and Social Stratification

1. Ralph Linton, *The Study of Man* (New York: Appleton-Century Crofts, 1936); Cecil Clare North, *Social Differentiation* (Chapel Hill: University of North Carolina Press, 1926).
2. Cf. T. H. Marshall, *Citizenship and Social Class* (Cambridge: Cambridge University Press, 1950), pp. 96–97; and Kingsley Davis, *Human Society* (New York: Macmillan, 1949), pp. 364–365.
3. Cf. Gunnar Landtman, *The Origin of the Inequality of Social Classes* (Chicago: University of Chicago Press, 1938), Chap. 1; and Melville J. Herskovits, *Economic Anthropology* (New York: Knopf, 1952), Chap. 18.
4. L. T. Hobhouse, *Morals in Evolution* (New York: Henry Holt and Co., 1906), I, 284.
5. For treatments of the interconnections between economic and noneconomic phenomena, see Wilbert E. Moore, *Economy and Society,* Studies in Sociology (New York: Random House, 1955); and Neil J. Smelser, *The Sociology of Economic Life* (Englewood Cliffs, N.J.: Prentice-Hall, 1965).

Chapter II Historical Development of Social Stratification

1. Marshall Sahlins, *Stratification in Polynesia* (Seattle: University of Washington Press, 1958); M. G. Smith, "Pre-Industrial Stratification Systems," in Neil J. Smelser and S. M. Lipset (eds.), *Social Structure and Mobility in Economic Development* (Chicago: Aldine, 1966); Irving Goldman, "Status Rivalry and Cultural Evolution in Polynesia," *American Anthropologist,* 57, 4 (1955), 680–697; Irving Goldman, "The Evolution of Polynesian Societies," in Stanley Diamond (ed.), *Culture in History* (New York: Columbia University Press, 1960), pp. 687–712; and Morton Fried, "On the Evolution of Social Stratification and the State," in Diamond (ed.), *ibid.,* pp. 713–731.
2. Cf. Gordon Childe, *What Happened in History* (Baltimore: Penguin, 1946), pp. 82 ff.; and Ralph Turner, *The Great Cultural Traditions* (New York: McGraw-Hill, 1941), I, 286 ff.
3. Cf. Turner, *op. cit.,* p. 296.
4. *Ibid.,* p. 296.
5. *Ibid.,* p. 297.
6. *Ibid.,* p. 185.
7. Childe, *op. cit.,* p. 111.
8. Turner, *op. cit.,* pp. 302–305.
9. Cf. Henri Pirenne, *Economic and Social History of Medieval Europe* (New York: Harcourt, Brace & World), p. 7.
10. *Ibid.*
11. Cf. Marc Bloch, *La Société Féodale: les classes et le gouvernment des hommes* (Paris: Michel, 1940), Chap. 4.
12. James W. Thompson: *An Economic and Social History of the Middle Ages* (New York: Century, 1928), p. 647.
13. *Ibid.,* pp. 675–676.
14. Cf. Paul Vinogradoff, *The Growth of the Manor* (New York: Macmillan, 1905), pp. 332–335.
15. Pirenne, *op. cit.,* p. 52.

Chapter III Dimensions of Social Stratification in Modern Society

1. The exposition presented in the next paragraphs is based essentially on an essay by the German sociologist Max Weber, translated by H. H. Gerth and C. Wright Mills, *From Max Weber: Essays in Sociology* (New York: Oxford University Press, 1946), pp. 180–195. For some more recent elaborations of Weber's theory, see Milton M. Gordon, "A System of Social Class Analysis," *The Drew University Bulletin,* 39 (August 1951); Seymour M. Lipset and Reinhard Bendix, "Social Status and Social Structure. A Re-examination of Data and Interpretations," *British Journal of Sociology,* 2 (June and September 1951), 150–168, 230–254; Hans Gerth and C. Wright Mills, *Character and Social Structure* (New York: Harcourt, Brace & World, 1953), Chap. 11; and Kurt Mayer, "The Theory of Social Classes," *Harvard Educational Review,* 23 (Summer 1953), 149–167, from which many of the above formulations are taken.
2. Gerth and Mills, *op. cit.,* p. 313.
3. Cf. Lipset and Bendix, *op. cit.,* p. 249.
4. *Ibid.,* pp. 249–250.
5. Gerth and Mills, *op. cit.,* p. 317.
6. For an analysis of the concept of countervailing power, see John K. Galbraith, *American Capitalism* (Boston: Houghton Mifflin, 1952).
7. Cf. Gerth and Mills, *op. cit.,* pp. 328–330; and Lipset and Bendix, *op. cit.,* pp. 249–254.
8. Gunnar Myrdal, *An American Dilemma* (New York: Harper & Row, 1944).
9. For summaries of much of this research, see Thomas E. Lasswell, *Class and Stratum* (Boston: Houghton Mifflin, 1965); Harold M. Hodges, *Social Stratification* (New York: Harcourt, Brace & World, 1967); Reinhard Bendix and S. M. Lipset (eds.), *Class, Status, and Power,* 2d ed. (New York: Free Press, 1966).
10. Angus Campbell, *et al., The American Voter* (New York: Wiley, 1960).

Chapter IV Class in American Society: The Distribution of Life Chances

1. Survey Research Center, *1960 Survey of Consumer Finances* (Ann Arbor, Mich.: Braun Brumfield, 1961), Table 7-4, p. 126.
2. *Ibid.*, Table 7-2, p. 124.
3. Robert J. Lampman, *The Share of Top Wealth Holders in National Wealth, 1922–1956* (Princeton, N.J.: Princeton University Press, 1962), pp. 191–195.
4. A reasonable cutoff point for the "poverty line" in the United States in the early 1960s may be set at an annual income of $3,000 to $3,500 or less for an urban family of four. On this basis around 50 million people would be considered impoverished. See Michael Harrington, *The Other America* (New York: Macmillan, 1962), Appendix, pp. 175–191; Herman P. Miller, *Rich Man, Poor Man* (New York, Crowell, 1964), Chap. V.
5. See, e.g., Frederick L. Allen, *The Big Change* (New York: Harper & Row, 1952); Joseph J. Spengler, "Changes in Income Distribution and Social Stratification: A Note," *American Journal of Sociology,* 59 (November 1953), 253.
6. Aaron Antonovsky, "Social Class, Life Expectancy and Overall Mortality," *Milbank Memorial Fund Quarterly,* 45 (April 1967), 31–73.
7. Evelyn M. Kitagawa and Philip M. Hauser, "Social and Economic Differentials in Mortality, United States, 1960." Paper presented at annual meeting of the Population Association of America, New York, April 1966.
8. U. S. National Center for Health Statistics, Series 10, No. 17, May 1965, Table 17, p. 28.
9. *Ibid.,* p. 10.
10. *Ibid.,* Table C, p. 8. For a different interpretation of such figures, see Charles Kadushin, "Social Class and the Experience of Ill Health," *Sociological Inquiry,* 34 (Winter 1964), 67–80.
11. Cf. August B. Hollingshead and Frederick C. Redlich, "Social

Stratification and Psychiatric Disorders," *American Sociological Review,* 18 (April 1953), 163–169; and their *Social Class and Mental Illness* (New York, Wiley, 1958). See also Jerome K. Meyers and Leslie Schaffer, "Social Stratification and Psychiatric Practice: A Study of an Out-Patient Clinic," *American Sociological Review,* 19 (June 1954), 307–310, which shows not only that an individual's chance for receiving clinical treatment is related to his class position, but also the character of his subsequent clinical experience: the higher an individual's class position, the better his chances for treatment by highly trained psychiatrists and for intensive therapy over a long period of time.

12. U.S. Census of the Population: 1960, Vol. II, *Subject Reports,* PC (2)-5B.
13. Miller, *op. cit.,* p. 162.
14. *Ibid.,* pp. 163–164.
15. *Ibid.,* p. 165.
16. Raymond A. Mulligan, "Socio-economic Background and College Enrollment," *American Sociological Review,* 16 (April 1951), 188–196.
17. James S. Davie, "Social Class Factors and School Attendance," *Harvard Educational Review,* 23 (Summer 1953), 175–185.
18. *Ibid.,* pp. 184–185.
19. August B. Hollingshead, *Elmtown's Youth* (New York: Wiley, 1949), Chap. 8.
20. W. Lloyd Warner, Robert J. Havighurst, and Martin B. Loeb, *Who Shall Be Educated?* (New York: Harper, 1944), Chap. 6.
21. Joseph A. Kahl, "Educational and Occupational Aspirations of 'Common Man' Boys," *Harvard Educational Review,* 23 (Summer 1953), 186–203; see also William H. Sewell, A. O. Haller, and M. A. Strauss, "Social Status and Educational and Occupational Aspiration," *American Sociological Review,* 22 (February 1957), 67–73; Brian Jackson and Dennis Marsden, *Education and the Working Class* (New York: Monthly Review Press, 1962).
22. W. Lloyd Warner and Paul S. Lunt, *The Social Life of a Modern Community* (New Haven, Conn.: Yale University Press, 1941), pp. 375–376.
23. *Ibid.,* p. 373.

24. John Useem, Pierre Tangent, and Ruth Useem, "Stratification in a Prairie Town," *American Sociological Review,* 7 (June 1942), 341.
25. Cf. Edwin H. Sutherland, *White Collar Crime* (New York: Holt, Rinehart and Winston, 1961); and Marshall B. Clinard, *The Black Market* (New York: Holt, Rinehart and Winston, 1952).

Chapter V Prestige, Style of Life, and Status Groups in American Society

1. The following is a list of only some of the most widely known community studies: Robert S. Lynd and Helen M. Lynd, *Middletown* (New York: Harcourt, Brace & World, 1929) and *Middletown in Transition* (New York: Harcourt, Brace & World, 1937); W. Lloyd Warner and Paul S. Lunt, *The Social Life of a Modern Community* (New Haven, Conn.: Yale University Press, 1941); Allison Davis, Burleigh B. Gardner, and Mary R. Gardner, *Deep South* (Chicago: University of Chicago Press, 1941); James West, *Plainville, U.S.A.* (New York: Columbia University Press, 1945); August B. Hollingshead, *Elmtown's Youth* (New York: Wiley, 1949); W. Lloyd Warner and associates, *Democracy in Jonesville* (New York: Harper & Row 1949); Art Gallaher, Jr., *Plainville: Fifteen Years Later* (New York: Columbia University Press, 1961). For a bibliography of recent studies, see John Walton, "Discipline, Method, and Community Power: A Note on the Sociology of Knowledge," *American Sociological Review,* 31 (October 1966), 684–689.
2. Mirra Komarovsky, "The Voluntary Association of Urban Dwellers," *American Sociological Review,* 11 (December 1946), 688–689. See also the more recent work, Murry Hausknecht, *The Joiners* (New York: Bedminster Press, 1962).
3. Warner and Lunt, *op. cit.,* Chap. 16.
4. Floyd Dotson, "Patterns of Voluntary Association among Urban Working Class Families," *American Sociological Review, 16* (October 1951), 689.
5. *Ibid.,* pp. 690–692.
6. Cf. Liston Pope, "Religion and the Class Structure," *Annals*

of the American Academy of Political and Social Science, 256 (March 1948), 84–91. See also Herbert W. Schneider, *Religion in 20th Century America* (Cambridge, Mass.: Harvard University Press, 1952), pp. 223–238. This tendency seems to have lessened in recent years. See, for example, N. J. Demerath III, *Social Class in American Protestantism* (Chicago: Rand McNally, 1965).

7. Cf. Davis, Gardner, and Gardner, *op. cit.,* Chap. 7; and Warner and Lunt, *op. cit.,* pp. 350–355.
8. Edward O. Laumann, *Prestige and Association in an Urban Community* (Indianapolis: Bobbs Merrill, 1966).
9. Cf. Thorstein Veblen, *The Theory of the Leisure Class* (New York: Macmillan, 1899); and Cleveland Amory, *The Last Resorts* (New York: Harper & Row 1952).
10. A classic fictional account of the frustrated attempts of an upper-middle-class businessman to win social acceptance by the upper class is, of course, Sinclair Lewis' *Babbitt,* published in 1922. Since then, this theme has been stressed in many American novels.
11. Cf. Martin B. Loeb, "Implications of Status Differentiation for Personal and Social Development," *Harvard Educational Review,* 23 (Summer 1953), 168–174.
12. See especially John H. Goldthorpe and David Lockwood, "Affluence and the British Class Structure," *Sociological Review,* 2 (1963), 133–163; David Lockwood, "The 'New Working Class,' " *European Journal of Sociology,* I, 2 (1960), 248–259; and T. B. Bottomore, *Classes in Modern Society* (New York: Pantheon Books, 1966). Although these critiques are based mainly on studies of European societies, they are relevant to American society as well.
13. See, for example, John E. Anderson, *The Young Child in the Home* (New York: Appleton-Century-Crofts, 1936); W. Allison Davis and Robert J. Havighurst, *Father of the Man* (Boston: Houghton Mifflin, 1947); and Evelyn M. Duvall, "Conceptions of Parenthood," *American Journal of Sociology,* 52 (November 1946), 193–203.
14. Urie Bronfenbrenner, "Socialization and Social Class Through Time and Space," in E. E. Maccoby, T. M. Newcomb, and E. L. Hartley (eds.), *Readings in Social Psychology,* 3d ed. (New York: Holt, Rinehart and Winston, 1958), pp. 400–425.

15. Cf. "Social Class and Parent-Child Relationships," *American Journal of Sociology,* 68 (January 1963), 471–480.
16. Cf. Alfred C. Kinsey, Wardell B. Pomeroy, and Clyde E. Martin, *Sexual Behavior in the Human Male* (Philadelphia: Saunders, 1948), Chaps. 10 and 11; and Alfred C. Kinsey *et al., Sexual Behavior in the Human Female* (Philadelphia: Saunders, 1953), especially Chaps. 7 and 8. In the latter volume the hypothesis is presented that females are less susceptible than males to social pressures insofar as their sexual conduct is concerned.
17. See, for example, William Foote Whyte, "A Slum Sex Code," *American Journal of Sociology,* 49 (July 1943), 24–31; and Hollingshead, *op. cit.,* Chap. 16. For a brief review of recent changes among youth, see Mervin B. Freedman, *The College Experience* (San Francisco: Jossey Press, 1967), Part III.
18. Hollingshead, *op. cit.,* Chap. 9.
19. Cf. Richard Centers, "Marital Selection and Occupational Strata," *American Journal of Sociology,* 54 (May 1949), 530–535; and August B. Hollingshead, "Cultural Factors in the Selection of Marriage Mates," *American Sociological Review,* 15 (October 1950), 619–627.
20. Cf. August B. Hollingshead, "Class Differences in Family Stability," *Annals of the American Academy of Political and Social Science,* 272 (November 1950), 40–41.
21. *Ibid.,* pp. 42–43.
22. *Ibid.,* pp. 45–46.
23. For a discussion of this usage of "caste," see Robert M. MacIver and Charles H. Page, *Society: An Introductory Analysis* (New York: Holt, Rinehart and Winston, 1949), pp. 394 ff. For an excellent discussion of the "color line" in general, see Tamotsu Shibutani and K. M. Kwan, *Ethnic Stratification* (New York: Wiley, 1966).
24. Herman P. Miller, *Rich Man, Poor Man* (New York: Crowell, 1964), Chap. VI.
25. Cf. Davis, Gardner, and Gardner, *op. cit.;* John Dollard, *Caste and Class in a Southern Town* (New York: Harper & Row, 1937); Hortense Powdermaker, *After Freedom* (New York: Viking, 1939); St. Clair Drake and Horace R. Cayton, *Black Metropolis* (New York: Harcourt, Brace & World, 1945); and

E. Franklin Frazier, *The Negro in the United States,* rev. ed. (New York: Macmillan, 1957), Chap. 12.

26. Frazier, *op. cit.,* p. 303.
27. Cf. Elin L. Anderson, *We Americans* (Cambridge, Mass.: Harvard University Press, 1937); W. Lloyd Warner and Leo Srole, *The Social Systems of American Ethnic Groups* (New Haven, Conn.: Yale University Press, 1945); and W. Lloyd Warner and associates, *op. cit.,* Chap. 11.
28. An intensive examination of the background characteristics of the top social prestige group in an upstate New York city of 50,000 population came to this unequivocal conclusion: "In Northtown, membership in an ethnic group is the most definite and clearly defined status which acts as a block or preventive of acceptance into elite status." Leila Calhoun Deasy, "Social Mobility in Northtown" (unpublished Ph.D. dissertation, Cornell University, 1953), p. 139. See also Anderson, *op. cit.,* Chap. 8; and Warner and Srole, *op. cit.,* Chap. 5. It is true, of course, that occasionally individuals are successful in breaking away entirely from their ethnic group, thereby winning social acceptance in "Old American" circles.
29. August B. Hollingshead, "Trends in Social Stratification: A Case Study," *American Sociological Review,* 17 (December 1952), 686.
30. Ruby Jo Reeves Kennedy, "Single or Triple Melting-Pot? Intermarriage Trends in New Haven, 1870–1940," *American Journal of Sociology,* 49 (January 1944), 331–339; Will Herberg, *Protestant—Catholic—Jew* (Garden City, N.Y.: Doubleday, 1955).
31. Milton M. Gordon, *Assimilation in American Life* (New York: Oxford University Press, 1964), Chaps. 5 and 7; Nathan Glazer and Daniel P. Moynihan, *Beyond the Melting Pot* (Cambridge, Mass.: M.I.T. and Harvard University Presses, 1963).
32. Gerhard E. Lenski, "American Social Classes: Statistical Strata or Social Groups," *American Journal of Sociology,* 58 (September 1952), 144. See also Gregory P. Stone and William H. Form, "Instabilities in Status: The Problem of Hierarchy in the Community Study of Status Arrangements," *American Sociological Review,* 18 (April 1953), 149–162.

Chapter VI The Structure of Power: Class, Formal Authority, and Informal Controls

1. A. A. Berle, Jr., "Economic Power and the Free Society," in Andrew Hacker (ed.), *The Corporation Take-Over* (New York: Harper & Row, 1964), Chap. 5.
2. John K. Galbraith, *The New Industrial State* (Boston: Houghton Mifflin, 1967).
3. These communities are reported, respectively, in the following volumes: Floyd Hunter, *Community Power Structure* (Chapel Hill: University of North Carolina Press, 1953); Robert S. Lynd and Helen M. Lynd, *Middletown in Transition* (New York: Harcourt, Brace & World, 1937); August B. Hollingshead, *Elmtown's Youth* (New York: Wiley, 1949); and Arthur J. Vidich and Joseph Bensman, *Small Town in Mass Society* (Garden City, N.Y.: Doubleday, 1960).
4. Hunter, *op. cit.*, pp. 75–76.
5. *Ibid.*, p. 65.
6. *Ibid.*, pp. 81, 102–103.
7. *Ibid.*, pp. 161–163.
8. *Ibid.*, pp. 248 ff.
9. Lynd and Lynd, *op. cit.*, Chap. 3.
10. *Ibid.*, pp. 91–101.
11. Hollingshead, *op. cit.*, Chap. 5.
12. Vidich and Bensman, *op. cit.*
13. *Ibid.*, pp. 100–101.
14. John Walton, "Discipline, Method, and Community Power: A Note on the Sociology of Knowledge," *American Sociological Review*, 31 (October 1966), 684–689.
15. Robert A. Dahl, "A Critique of the Ruling Elite Model," *American Political Science Review*, 52 (June 1958), 463–469; Nelson W. Polsby, "How to Study Power: The Pluralist Alternative," *Journal of Politics*, 22 (August 1960), 474–484; Raymond E. Wolfinger, "Reputation and Reality in the Study of Community Power," *American Sociological Review*, 27 (June 1962), 362–376.

16. William V. D'Antonio and Eugene Erickson, "The Reputational Technique as a Measure of Community Power," *American Sociological Review,* 27 (June 1962), 362–376.
17. Cf. Temporary National Economic Committee, *Economic Power and Political Pressures,* Monograph No. 26 (Washington, D.C.: Government Printing Office, 1941).
18. C. Wright Mills, *The Power Elite* (New York: Oxford University Press, 1956).
19. *Ibid.,* p. 11.
20. See, for example, Talcott Parsons, *Structure and Process in Modern Societies* (New York: Free Press, 1960), Chap. 6; T. B. Bottomore, *Elites and Society* (New York: Basic Books, 1964), pp. 27–30; Suzanne Keller, *Beyond the Ruling Class: Strategic Elites in Modern Society* (New York: Random House, 1963), pp. 108–109; and Arnold M. Rose, *The Power Structure* (New York: Oxford University Press, 1967).
21. Floyd Hunter, *Top Leadership, U.S.A.* (Chapel Hill, University of North Carolina Press, 1959).
22. *Ibid.,* p. 11.
23. Cf. David B. Truman, *The Governmental Process* (New York: Knopf, 1951), p. 258. For an opposing point of view, see Robert A. Brady, *Business as a System of Power* (New York: Columbia University Press, 1943).
24. David Riesman, Nathan Glazer, and Reuel Denny, *The Lonely Crowd* (Garden City, N.Y.: Doubleday Anchor Book A 16, 1953), Chap. 10.
25. *Ibid.,* p. 247.
26. *Op. cit.*
27. *Ibid.,* p. 20.
28. *Ibid.,* p. 277.
29. *Op. cit.,* p. 118.

Chapter VII Class Awareness and Class Consciousness

1. See, for example, Arthur W. Kornhauser, "Analysis of 'Class' Structure of Contemporary American Society: Psychological Bases of Class Division," in George W. Hartmann and Theodore Newcomb (eds.), *Industrial Conflict* (New York: Cordon,

1939), pp. 230–250; Alfred Winslow Jones, *Life, Liberty, and Property* (Philadelphia: Lippincott, 1941); Richard Centers, *The Psychology of Social Classes* (Princeton, N.J.: Princeton University Press, 1949); Herman M. Case, "An Independent Test of the Interest-Group Theory of Social Class," *American Sociological Review,* 17 (December 1952), 751–755; and Oscar Glantz, "Class Consciousness and Political Solidarity," *American Sociological Review,* 23 (August 1958), 375–383.

2. Centers, *op. cit.,* Table 9, p. 60.
3. Case, *op. cit.*
4. Cf. Kornhauser, *op. cit.,* and Centers, *op. cit.,* pp. 65–69. See also Paul F. Lazarsfeld, Bernard Berelson, and Hazel Gaudet, *The People's Choice* (New York: Duell, Sloan & Pearce, 1947); Gerhart H. Saenger, "Social Status and Political Behavior," *American Journal of Sociology,* 51 (September 1945), 103–113; Angus Campbell, Gerald Gurin, and Warren E. Miller, *The Voter Decides* (New York: Harper & Row, 1945); Alfred DeGrazia, *The Western Public: 1952 and Beyond* (Stanford, Calif.: Stanford University Press, 1954); Bernard R. Berelson, Paul F. Lazarsfeld, and William McPhee, *Voting* (Chicago: University of Chicago Press, 1954); Angus Campbell *et al., The American Voter* (New York: Wiley, 1960); and Robert R. Alford, *Party and Society* (Chicago: Rand McNally, 1963).
5. Glantz, *op. cit.*
6. Campbell *et al., op. cit.;* Alford, *op. cit.*
7. Alford, *op. cit.,* Chap. 8.
8. S. Stansfeld Sargent, "Class and Class Consciousness in a California Town," *Social Problems,* 1 (June 1953), 22–27.
9. Neal Gross, "Social Class Identification in the Urban Community," *American Sociological Review,* 18 (August 1953), 399.
10. *Ibid.,* p. 402.
11. C. Wright Mills, *White Collar* (New York: Oxford University Press, 1951), p. 325.
12. Alford, *op. cit.,* p. 219.
13. Cf. Allison Davis, Burleigh B. Gardner, and Mary R. Gardner, *Deep South* (Chicago: University of Chicago Press, 1941), pp. 63–73; James West, *Plainville, U.S.A.* (New York: Columbia University Press, 1945), pp. 128–133; and W. Lloyd

Warner, Marchia Meeker, and Kenneth Eells, *Social Class in America* (Chicago: Science Research Associates, 1949), Chap. 3.

14. We are indebted to the excellent analysis contained in Morris Rosenberg, "Perceptual Obstacles to Class Consciousness," *Social Forces,* 32 (October 1953), 22–27. For other perceptive discussions of the lack of class consciousness, see Robin M. Williams, Jr., *American Society* (New York: Knopf, 1960), pp. 115–135; and R. M. MacIver and Charles H. Page, *Society* (New York: Holt, Rinehart and Winston, 1949), pp. 358–364.
15. See Ely Chinoy, *Automobile Workers and The American Dream* (New York: Random House, 1955), for an interesting analysis of both the persistence of the "dream" and its weakening in this group.

Chapter VIII Social Mobility

1. Cf. Richard Centers, "Occupational Mobility of Urban Occupational Strata," *American Sociological Review,* 12 (April 1948), 197–203; and National Opinion Research Center, "Jobs and Occupations: A Popular Evaluation," *Opinion News,* 9 (September 1947), 12–13.
2. Cf. Percy E. Davidson and H. Dewey Anderson, *Occupational Mobility in an American Community* (Stanford, Calif.: Stanford University Press, 1937); Natalie Rogoff, *Recent Trends in Occupational Mobility* (New York: Free Press, 1953); Seymour M. Lipset and Reinhard Bendix, "Social Mobility and Occupational Career Patterns," *American Journal of Sociology,* 57 (January–March 1952), 366–374, 494–504; Reinhard Bendix, Seymour M. Lipset, and F. Theodore Malm, "Social Origins and Occupational Career Patterns," *Industrial and Labor Relations Review,* 7 (January 1954), 246–261; and Godfrey Hochbaum, John G. Darley, E. D. Monachesi, and Charles Bird, "Socio-Economic Variables in a Large City," *American Journal of Sociology,* 61 (1955), 31–38.
3. Hochbaum, Darley, Monachesi, and Bird, *op. cit.*
4. See Seymour M. Lipset and Reinhard Bendix, *Social Mobility in Industrial Society* (Berkeley: University of California Press, 1960), p. 88.

5. Bendix, Lipset, and Malm, *op. cit.*, pp. 251–252.
6. Cf. Davidson and Anderson, *op. cit.;* and Lipset and Bendix, *op. cit.*
7. Lipset and Bendix, *op. cit.*
8. Davidson and Anderson, *op. cit.*, p. 180.
9. F. W. Taussig and C. S. Joslyn, *American Business Leaders* (New York, Macmillan, 1932).
10. W. Lloyd Warner and James C. Abegglen, *Occupational Mobility in American Business and Industry, 1928–1952* (Minneapolis: University of Minnesota Press, 1955).
11. William Miller (ed.), *Men in Business* (New York: Harper Torchbooks, 1962), Chaps. VII, XI, XII, and XIII; Mabel Newcomer, *The Big Business Executive* (New York: Columbia University Press, 1955).
12. Suzanne Keller, *Beyond the Ruling Class* (New York: Random House, 1963), Appendix II.
13. Cf. James West, *Plainville, U.S.A.* (New York: Columbia University Press, 1945), pp. 134–141; and W. Lloyd Warner and associates; *Democracy in Jonesville* (New York: Harper & Row, 1949), Chap. 4.
14. For example: Booth Tarkington, *The Magnificent Ambersons;* Christopher LaFarge, *The Wilsons;* Christopher Morley, *Kitty Foyle;* John P. Marquand, *Point of No Return;* and Hamilton Basso, *The View from Pompey's Head.*
15. Cf. Leila Calhoun Deasy, "Social Mobility in Northtown" (unpublished Ph.D. dissertation, Cornell University, 1953).
16. *Ibid.*, p. 225.
17. *Ibid.*, pp. 227–228.
18. *Ibid.*, p. 232.
19. See Seymour M. Lipset and Reinhard Bendix, "Ideological Equalitarianism and Social Mobility in the United States," in *Transactions of the Second World Congress of Sociology,* Vol. II: *Social Stratification and Social Mobility* (London: International Sociological Association, 1954), pp. 34–54; and William Petersen, "Is America Still the Land of Opportunity?" *Commentary,* 16 (November 1953), 477–486.
20. See, for example, Rogoff, *op. cit.*, Chap. 5.
21. See, for example, J. O. Hertzler, "Some Tendencies toward a Closed Class System in the United States," *Social Forces,* 30 (March 1952), 313–323; August B. Hollingshead, "Trends in

Social Stratification: A Case Study," *American Sociological Review,* 17 (December 1952), 679–686; Gideon Sjoberg, "Are Social Classes in America Becoming More Rigid?" *American Sociological Review,* 16 (December 1951), 775–783; William Petersen, *op. cit.;* Seymour M. Lipset and Reinhard Bendix, *op. cit.;* and Ely Chinoy, "Social Mobility Trends in the United States," *American Sociological Review,* 20 (April 1955), 180–186.

22. Rogoff, *op. cit.*
23. Herman P. Miller, *Rich Man, Poor Man* (New York: Crowell, 1964), p. 29.
24. *Ibid.,* Chap. IV.
25. Claude Julien, *L'Empire Americain* (Paris: Grasset, 1968); William A. Williams, *The Contours of American History* (Chicago: Quadrangle, 1966); Fred J. Cook, *The Warfare State* (New York: Macmillan, 1962); David Harowitz, *The Free World Colossus* (New York: Hill & Wang, 1965).

Selected Readings

Baltzell, E. Digby. *Philadelphia Gentlemen.* New York: Free Press, 1958. A study of the making of a national upper class.

Bendix, Reinhard, and Seymour Martin Lipset. *Class, Status and Power.* 2d ed. New York: Free Press, 1966. A highly useful collection of readings covering many aspects of social stratification in the United States and other countries.

Blau, Peter M., and O. Dudley Duncan. *The American Occupational Structure.* New York: Wiley, 1967. An important survey of occupational structure and mobility in the United States.

Bottomore, T. B. *Classes in Modern Society.* New York: Pantheon Books, 1966. An excellent discussion of contemporary issues in stratification theory and research.

Centers, Richard. *The Psychology of Social Classes.* Princeton, N.J.: Princeton University Press, 1949. An empirical investigation of the relationship between subjective and objective indexes of class, based on a cross section of the national population and employing the technique of the public opinion poll.

Coleman, James S., *et al. Equality of Educational Opportunity.* Washington, D.C.: United States Government Printing Office, 1966. A definitive survey of the current level of educational opportunity in the United States.

Dahrendorf, Ralf. *Class and Class Conflict in Industrial Society.* Stanford, Calif.: Stanford University Press, 1959. A critique of Marxian and of structural-functional class theories and an attempt to develop a new theory of class conflict.

Davis, Allison, Burleigh B. Gardner, and Mary R. Gardner. *Deep South.* Chicago: University of Chicago Press, 1941. A detailed description of social class and the Negro "caste" in the American South, based upon a study of "Old City."

Domhoff, G. William. *Who Rules America?* Englewood Cliffs, N.J.: Prentice-Hall, 1967. A reanalysis of some important studies and theories of power in America.

Gordon, Milton M. *Social Class in American Sociology.* Durham, N. C.: Duke University Press, 1958. Critical analysis of contemporary American literature on stratification.

Harrington, Michael. *The Other America: Poverty in the United States.* New York: Macmillan, 1962. The book that "rediscovered" poverty for Americans and helped initiate the current governmental "War on Poverty."

Hollingshead, August B. *Elmtown's Youth.* New York: Wiley, 1949. A revealing study of the impact of social stratification on adolescents in a small Midwestern community.

Hunter, Floyd. *Community Power Structure.* Chapel Hill: University of North Carolina Press, 1953. One of the first attempts to investigate empirically the power structure of an American city.

Hutton, J. H. *Caste in India: Its Nature, Function, and Origins.* 2d ed. Cambridge: Cambridge University Press, 1951. A systematic treatise on the Indian caste system.

Landtman, Gunnar. *The Origin of the Inequality of the Social Classes.* Chicago: University of Chicago Press, 1938. A comparative and evolutionary treatment of social stratification in primitive societies.

Lenski, Gerhard E. *Power and Privilege: A Theory of Social Stratification.* New York: McGraw-Hill, 1966. A critical analysis of stratification theory, based upon an examination of a wide range of literature and historical data.

Lipset, Seymour Martin, and Reinhard Bendix. *Social Mobility in Industrial Society.* Berkeley and Los Angeles: University of California Press, 1950. A comparative analysis of social mobility based on several empirical studies.

Marshall, T. H. *Citizenship and Social Class and Other Essays.* Cambridge: Cambridge University Press, 1950. Contains a cogent theoretical discussion of the nature and function of social stratification by a British scholar.

Marx, Karl, and Friedrich Engels. *Manifesto of the Communist Party.* New York: International Publishers, 1934. Contains the statement of the well-known theory of class struggle, presented in the form of a program for political action. Although never fully developed and not adequately clarified conceptually, Marx's class theory is a sociological classic.

Mills, C. Wright. *The Power Elite.* New York: Oxford University Press, 1956. A provocative analysis of the power structure of the United States.

Page, Charles H. *Class and American Sociology: From Ward to Ross.* New York: Shocken Books, 1969. Analyzes the class theories of pioneer American sociologists.

Porter, John. *The Vertical Mosaic: An Analysis of Social Class and Power in Canada.* Toronto: University of Toronto Press, 1965. The most thorough and penetrating study of stratification in a modern Western society.

Transactions of the Second World Congress of Sociology, Vol. II (1954), and *Transactions of the Third World Congress of Sociology,* Vols. III and IV (1956). London: International Sociological Association. Collections of papers of international scope concerned with a wide range of theoretical problems and empirical studies on a world-wide scale.

Veblen, Thorstein. *The Theory of the Leisure Class.* New York: Macmillan, 1899. A classic statement of the invidious aspect of social stratification, which remains especially relevant to the study of the American scene.

Warner, W. Lloyd, and Paul S. Lunt. *The Social Life of a Modern Community.* New Haven, Conn.: Yale University Press, 1941. A pioneer empirical study of the status hierarchy in a New England town.

Warner, W. Lloyd, Marchia Meeker, and Kenneth Eells. *Social Class in America.* Chicago: Science Research Associates, 1949. A methodological proposal for the empirical study of community stratification, though with many weaknesses.

Weber, Max, *From Max Weber: Essays in Sociology.* Edited and translated by H. H. Gerth and C. W. Mills. New York: Oxford University Press, 1946, pp. 180–195. A distinguished attempt to clarify the basic concepts of social stratification in the classical European tradition.

Index

Abegglen, J. C., 141
Achievement, 5, 6
Alford, R., 128, 131
Amory, C., 93
Ascription, 5, 19
Aristocracy, 24, 28, 29, 34, 35, 37, 41; *see also* Ruling class, Upper class, Elite
Associations (and class participation), 87–91
Authority, 7, 9, Chapter VI

Bensman, J., 115
Berle, A. A., 110
Black power, 104
Bottomore, T. B., 124
Bourgeoisie, 38, 39, 41, 135
Brahmans, 31, 32
Bronfenbrenner, U., 98

Campbell, A., 55
Capitalist society, 67, 110, 134
Case, H. M., 127
Caste, 14, 30–33, 102
  defined, 13
Centers, R., 127, 130, 140
Class, 13, 30, 40, 41, 43, 47
  conflict, 155
  consumption patterns, 91 ff.
  defined, 15, 44–45
  differentials, Chapter IV
  family patterns, 96 ff.
  perpetuation of, 51–60
  sex behavior, 96 ff.
  value orientations, 91 ff., 154
Class consciousness, 45–46, Chapter VII
  and awareness, 126 ff.
  and identification, 129 ff.
  and the American dream, 134 ff.

Clergy (medieval), 36, 37

D'Antonio, W. V., 118
Differentiation, 4 ff., 19, 23
Discrimination, 103 ff., 147

Educational opportunity, 59, 73–79, 147–148
Elites, 82, 106, 111 ff., 123, 128, 141, 142; *see also* Aristocracy, Ruling class, Upper class
Embourgeoisment thesis, 95–96
Equality of opportunity, 7, 8, 17, 33, 62, 63, 75, 129, 130
Erickson, E., 118
Estate, 13, 14, 26, 27, 30, 33–41, 60
  definition, 34
Ethnic groups, 102 ff., 135

Family
  class differentials in behavior, 96 ff.
  and ranking system, 10, 19–22

Glantz, O., 128, 131

Harrington, M., 151
Hobhouse, L. T., 12
Hunter, F., 116, 117, 120, 122

Ideology, 43, 55, 62, 63, 121
  and mass media, 120–121
Income distribution, 63 ff., 149
  and education, 74–75
  relative shares, 69–70
"Income revolution," 151–152
Institutionalized inequality, 21, 22, Chapter IV
Interaction differentials, 52, 56, 59, 90–91

Joslyn, C. S., 141
Justice (class differentials), 79–81

Keller, S., 123
Kinsey, A. C., 100

Laumann, E. O., 90
Legal protection (class differentials), 79–81
Legitimacy, crisis of, 110 ff.
Life chances, Chapter IV
  defined, 45
Life-style, 35, 43, 47, 48, 55, Chapter V
Lynd, R. S. and H. M., 113, 114

Marx, K., 124
Middle class, 40, 82 ff., 88 ff., 133, 145
Mills, C. W., 119, 122, 131
Mobility, 50–51, 58, 59, 135–136, Chapter VIII
  career, 138 ff.
  defined, 50
  and immigration, 146–147
  intergenerational, 138 ff.
  status, 143–144
Model of perpetuation of classes, 51–60
Myrdal, G., 52

Negro class structure, 104–105

Occupational structure, 65–67
  and mobility, 138 ff., 145–146
Opportunity structure, 58, 142
Outcastes, 31, 32

Peasants, 24 ff., 29, 34, 37, 38, 41
Personality differentials, 52, 56–57
Pluralist theory of power, 117–118, 122–124
Political attitudes, 91, 126 ff.
Poverty, 152
  "war on", 151

Power, 7, 9, 13, 19, 24, 26, 29, 30, 44, 49–50, Chapter VI, 153, 154,
community, 111 ff.
defined, 11, 49
institutionalized, 11
national structure, 118 ff.
techniques of study, 117–118
Prestige, 7, 12, 13, 29, 32, 44, 46, 50, Chapter V, 132 ff.
Proletariat, 135

Race, 102 ff., 135, 147
Rank society (primitive), 19
Relative deprivation, 151–152
Religious distinctions, 102 ff., 135
Riesman, D., 122, 123
Rogoff, N., 148
Ruling class, 24, 26, 29, 30, 40; *see also* Aristocracy, Elites, Upper class

Sahlins, M., 21, 22
Serfs, 24 ff., 29, 34, 37, 41
Slavery, 27, 28, 29
Social position, 5, 7, 8, 11
differentials, 52, 54
inheritance of, 139 ff., 154
Status, 10, 22, 48, 86 ff., 105–106, 153, 154
defined, 46
rivalry, 19
Status group, 47–49, Chapter V, 133
defined, 15, 46

Strata, 9, 10, 12
defined, 8
Stratification vs. differentiation, 5 ff.
defined, 8
dimensions of, 44 ff., 50
in Polynesia, 21–23
and town life, 23
trends, 148–155
Stratified society (primitive), 20
Subculture (class), 52, 55, 59, 91 ff.
Surplus, 12, 19, 24, 29

Taussig, F. W., 141
Traditional society, 18
Triple melting pot hypothesis, 106

Unstratified society, 16
Upper class, 82 ff., 88 ff., 133, 141; *see also* Aristocracy, Elites, Ruling class
Urban classes, 26, 27, 40

Veblen, T., 93
Vidich, A. J., 115
Voting, 55, 58, 128

Walton, J., 116, 117
Warner, W. L., 141
Wealth, 7, 13, 24, 29, 30, 154,
distribution of, 63 ff., 67
Working class, 26, 27, 29, 82 ff., 88 ff., 133, 145